Henri's War,

A Buchenwald Holocaust Story

A Survivor

Copyrighted © 2015

All rights reserved. Except as permitted under the U.S. copyright Act of 1976, no part of this publication may be reproduced, stored in a retrieval system, or transmitted in any form or by any means, electronic, mechanical, photocopying, recording, or otherwise, without written permission of the publisher.

ACKNOWLEDGMENTS

This book is a product of my experiences in Buchenwald. Without those experiences, I, a cabinet maker, never would have dreamt of writing a book. I am indebted to all my comrades in Buchenwald who revealed to me a depth of human feeling and a strength of spirit I did not know existed before my meeting with them.

What I really tried to tell in this book is something of their courage and then, kindness. Where I failed, the fault is entirely my own; where I succeeded, the credit is solely theirs.

FOREWORD

This is the story of a survivor, what he saw and felt during his Calvary from Antwerp to the Malin distribution camp in France and from there to the extermination camp of Buchenwald.

To say that this book contains the scenes of a twentieth-century Inferno may sound commonplace. Yet, every page of this book reminds one of Dante's Inferno, with one exception: the Inferno, the author writes about consumed the lives not of the sinful whom divine justice cast into the immortality of suffering.

This Inferno was thronged by millions, many of whom were babies and little children, mothers and young women who had hoped to become mothers. It was thronged with people who deserved their fates because they were men in the sense that God meant them to be. They were in Inferno because they were strong men and brave, the real heroes of our days. They were doomed because the Nazi super-race set up a different scale of values which regarded heroism as the greatest of sins and considered depravity the greatest of virtues. Reading this book one feels that the titanic Dante himself would have been staggered by the demented criminality the judges of the just displayed. This is the story of No. 22383 of Buchenwald, one of the millions who were doomed and one of the few who escaped. The spirit of many of the survivors was broken, but not the spirit of this prisoner. He has turned his experiences in Inferno into a work of abiding art. A mere number, he had the strength to remain an artist, observing his captors, his fellow-prisoners, life in the shadow of death. He gives us masterpieces of descriptive writing about persons, such as Anya, the guardian angel of the Malin camp, and about events, such as the appearance of the music band, playing joyous tunes, a hundred paces from the crematorium. Throughout, the writing is poignant, vibrant with humanity, a cry "de profundis" and a vow that it must never happen again. This book should be long remembered.

Contents

ACKNOWLEDGMENTS 3
FOREWORD 4
Contents 6
1 9
2 18
3 24
4 31
5 36
6 43
7 50
8 65
9 70
10 81
11 85
12 97
13 105
14 112
15 124
16 130
17 140
18 148
19 156
20 163

21	171
22	175
23	182
24	190
25	201
26	210
27	219
28	230
29	234
30	250
31	255
32	276
33	280
34	287
35	293
36	302
37	312
38	326
39	334

Never say, when the skies are heavy-laden,
That you are treading the last path . . .
Because, just as the skies will one day clear,
It will come, this longed-for hour
As with the rumble-beat of a drum . . .
And we will be here!

From a Concentration Camp Song

1

In the scale of human feeling nothing is more terrible than to watch your child's anguish. A child fears death more than an adult. My six-year-old son was no different from other children in this. His terror weighed more heavily upon my heart than my own dread of Nazi airmen who were machine-gunning the escaping thousands.

I remember an air raid during which Henri said to me, "Lie on top of me, Papa, so the flyer can't see me!"

I realized then how a child thinks. It is inconceivable that anything can happen to his father. His father is eternal, indestructible. A child fears death but he believes that adults are too strong to die.

How many times did we see the grinning faces of young German airmen as they swooped down upon the road? Theirs was not irresponsible cruelty. They were carrying out a tactical plan. The

Germans needed the roads. We civilians cluttered these roads.

Our bodies blocked their trucks and tanks, their guns, their supplies. Therefore they shot us.

But when we left the roads the airmen, forgetting tactics for the sake of sport, sought us out in the woods or the fields. They hunted us as people hunt the fox or the rabbit.

With twelve million others we shared the niceties of total war.

I was a Hungarian in Belgium. In the madness of those days it was quite logical, in fact it was normal, for a man and his child to be wandering in a strange country.

The Belgian people were without illusions. Many had survived a German occupation during World War I, but it was not long before they thought of the Kaiser as a savior in comparison to the Nazis. They knew how idle Hitler's promise was, to respect Belgian and Dutch neutrality. When Poland fell Belgium became a death cell in which an entire people awaited the execution of sentence.

It was not a long wait. Six months of Sitzkrieg on the Western Front ended. On Friday, May 10, 1940, without the unnecessary verbosity of a declaration of war, bombers leveled half the country, and the German Ambassador, with straight face and well-tailored dignity, informed Belgian Foreign Minister Spaak that "the German government, with this military action, desires to defend Belgium from attack by the French and the English, and to ensure Belgian independence."

My son and I hid from the bombs and the flaming buildings in the ancient city of Antwerp, our independence assured.

In the morning the bombing stopped. The Belgian Government issued a proclamation, describing the invasion and calling up men between the ages of sixteen and forty-two for military service. The same proclamation ordered the internment of Austrian and German nationals, including refugee Jews from these countries. The Jews were sent to France.

Overnight there was a new ruler in Belgium— panic. Thousands fled. Their mass departure was without plan or leadership. Their haven was

England but since they had no means of getting there, they fled toward the French border, the sea, Ostend.

Crowds of terrified civilians clogged the railway stations or massed on the roads leading out of Antwerp where they made a standing target for German machine guns.

Some of us did not join in the hysteria. We understood that a journey without plan or leadership was foolish. We decided to wait two or three days after which the development of the invasion would make clear what course to take. My son and I gathered with five other families as a group. We agreed to wait until Monday when the roads and railways might be more clear of panicky people.

By May 13th our group had increased to seven families—twenty-four persons. Most of the adults in the group were trade unionists, accustomed to organization. We gathered together a minimum of food and clothing since we would travel by foot and would have to carry the smaller children for long distances. In order to forestall the possibility of endless discussions, plans, and counterplans, we elected three of our number to obtain food and shelter on the pilgrimage, and to make binding decisions. Our destination was France, one hundred and ten kilometers away.

One hundred and ten kilometers is an hour's journey by automobile. A man can walk it in two days under peacetime conditions. But when there are children, German planes in the air, terror beyond each bend of the road, the trip may last longer than a man's life. We were lucky enough to find room on a freight train leaving Antwerp, but after it took us a bare forty kilometers it halted. The Germans had destroyed the tracks. It was night and we waited in the open while increasingly bad news arrived of the latest German advances. The Nazis were already at the gates of Antwerp and Brussels.

At six in the morning we joined other thousands on the road, and walked the entire day without incident. By Wednesday morning we were only fifty kilometers from the French border. Every minute the number of refugees increased, including Belgian soldiers who had thrown away their weapons. The very threat of the Blitz had disintegrated large sections of the Belgian Army.

The German planes arrived at eleven o'clock. We threw ourselves face down on the road. The young pilots, flying at a height of only twenty-five or thirty meters, I effortlessly slaughtered many. Seven minutes later the planes were gone. The blue sky was still serene although it looked on a road red and sticky with the blood of our new dead. Men and women screamed hysterically. A number of people went insane.

Our group escaped harm. We met again and decided to avoid the road. We entered the forest, made a tent of our blankets, and remained there in comparative safety until morning.

On Thursday we reached the French frontier where the chaos became ironical. We, who were fleeing to the refuge of France, met Frenchmen fleeing to Belgium because the Germans had broken through the Maginot Line. The following day the tide turned again, and all the refugees began to crowd back into France. We followed because it was impossible to go against the tide.

Frontier police were examining all the refugees who crossed the border. Of our group twenty were Czechs (in actuality Hungarians from Upper Hungary). The police let them pass. When they questioned me I stated that I was a Hungarian Jew—and they refused me admission! Jew or not, I was Hungarian, and therefore an enemy alien! Following me was a couple named Goldberger who gave their nationality as Rumanian. They were also refused entry as enemy aliens. We tried to explain the obvious truth that a Hungarian Jew or a Rumanian Jew was no more an enemy of France than a Czech Jew, but it was futile.

Some of our group that passed inspection, including many women, wanted to return with us, but we insisted that they go ahead. We turned to take again the bitter road on which we had come. My child began to cry. "Papa," he asked, "why don't we go with the others?"

I lied. I said that we and the Goldbergers were going to a better place where there would be no Germans, no armies, and no machine guns. Again we walked; again I took my boy of six along a road lined with overturned trucks and tanks, the careless bodies of the dead, the putrid odor of cadavers. We went toward Ostend, impelled by hopes of an impossible miracle that might provide us with a Channel crossing. We almost succeeded—but the planes caught up with us when we were only thirty kilometers from the sea.

We leaped into a stinking ditch, filled with dirt and slime, and when we emerged a few minutes later, covered from head to foot with filth, we were alive. Life was an achievement. Around us lay a fresh harvest of bodies. Worse than the dead were the agonized wounded, the despairing cries of the children, the harrowing screams of those whose only wounds were mental. I think that I myself lost my mind for a few minutes after that strafing.

Ahead of us was a bridge, and beyond that a forest that promised some safety. Since the bridge was without sentries we knew it had been mined. Tortured by thirst, we hurried toward it. Only a few hundred of us succeeded in crossing before it blew up. In the scant shelter of the forest we found fresh water; we drank and bathed ourselves. Then we dragged ourselves on until we reached the little town of Midelkerk where the Goldbergers, my son, and myself found shelter in a garage.

We did not know that we had begun a four-year flight from death.

2

War creates many fanciful contrasts. The next day we made the acquaintance of a well-to-do Polish Jew from Antwerp who invited us to move into a comfortable Midelkerk hotel where he was staying with his family. We accepted the invitation because it had become clear in the last twenty-four hours that there was no possibility of escape from this town. All we could do was wait—in comfort, if possible—for the Germans.

Our new friend took us to the most elaborate sea-side hotel in Midelkerk. In peacetime such elegance would have been impossible for me. It was a Cinderella dream tangled in a nightmare. The proprietor of the hotel had fled. I did not register. I paid nothing. I simply looked around, found a beautifully furnished room on the third floor, and occupied it. Henri threw himself upon the clean bed, stretched happily, and asked, "Can we stay here, Papa? Do we have to go any further?"

I said we would stay, and so we stayed, but whether it was to be for an hour or a week I could not know.

We had a lovely sea view from the window, and a private bath with running water. I gave Henri a thorough scrubbing and put him in the soft bed where he slept the sleep of complete exhaustion.

The hotel's restaurant was on the main floor, but since there was no one to prepare or serve food, we took what we needed from the pantry which was filled with the best of foods. For two hours we were at peace. There was no new word of the Germans. The Belgian Army had abandoned the town, the Germans were on their way in, and we reveled in the blessed limbo between the two events.

After resting and eating we went to the lobby to survey the deserted town, but when we reached the entrance we heard the air-raid sirens. Some forty of us were gathered in the hotel's glassed-in terrace, including a couple named Schwartz with whom I had become friendly. Before we had time to go to the safety of the basement, a bomb struck. Luckily it was a small one, and although it damaged the hotel's facade, our group received only indirect injuries, principally lacerations from flying glass, Mr. Schwartz, however, was badly cut up. We managed to get him to the hospital after discovering that the ambulance, miraculously enough, was still in service.

The minds of people were far less stable than their bodies in those horrible days. That bomb panicked many people. They fled, abandoning their possessions, scattering the contents of expensive trunks and suitcases. I took care of Mrs. Schwartz and stayed at the hotel with Henri because there was no sense in fleeing.

I remember most clearly the pantry of that hotel, and I remembered it even then, during the raid. After weeks of semi-starvation it was so unreal to come across the huge hams, thousands of cans of food, fruit, tons of frozen meat, which the proprietor had stored in expectation of a summer clientele that never arrived. After the raid I took Henri and Mrs. Schwartz down to that pantry where it was safer. "Would you like to eat?" I asked Henri.

Henri stared at the ceiling as though he could see the planes through it. He shook his head. He did not want food or comfort at the moment. He wanted to live.

Two hours later the ambulance returned from the hospital, bringing Schwartz who was weak from the loss of blood. The doctors had urged him to stay in the hospital but he wanted to remain with his wife. "What happens next?" he asked me.

"Next we wait here for the Germans," I said.

"Then we'll find out."

Since no bombers returned we concluded that the Germans were now very close. We went upstairs and stood on the sidewalk in front of the hotel. A few minutes later German tanks rolled down the street. Trucks followed, and then motorcycles. After the mechanized sections passed, the cavalry arrived. Mrs. Schwartz, who spoke German well, addressed a mounted soldier. "Bitte, Mein Herr," she said, "one of us is seriously injured and we have a child with us. We don't know what to do or where to go."

The German dismounted. He spoke to us very courteously, advising us to leave the town since the English would certainly open an artillery barrage from the sea. He even described in detail the route we should follow to Ghent. "You'll find a fleet of trucks in Ghent," he said. "The trucks will take the refugee's home—each to his own village."

It was surprisingly easy to speak to the soldier. We saw, with vast relief, that he was, after all, a man, a human being. His story sounded convincing since the Germans needed clear roads, especially now that their troops were mingled with the civilians, making mass machine-gunning impractical. Other soldiers gathered around our informant and they, too, were polite and helpful. Some even asked if we needed food or cigarettes.

We thanked them and returned to the hotel. After searching the basement, I found a hand-cart with rubber-tired wheels. I brought it upstairs and we put my wounded friend and my son in it, together with provisions. We took to the road once more and set off for Ghent.

We arrived in Ghent on May thirtieth. As the soldier had told us, there were many trucks in

Ghent, and German soldiers were filling them with refugees. We reported at the appropriate German head-quarters. They gave us a physical examination and re-dressed Schwartz's wounds. They, too, treated us well. They, too, were people, human beings. Then they put us on an enormous military truck, filled with other refugees, and we drove off as part of a fleet of about two hundred vehicles.

By half past eight one phase of our tortured flight was ended. We were back where we started from—in Antwerp.

3

Antwerp was dead. The German Army walked on its corpse.

After eight o'clock there were no civilians on the streets, but the Germans crowded the cafes. To my boy Henri, the death of this city was peace. In the Schwartz's home he said to me, "The war is over, isn't it, Papa? We don't have to go anyplace else, do we?"

I lied again. I said, "We are all right now, sonny. Go to sleep."

An old couple in the building said that the Germans had been behaving themselves, if you discounted the appropriation of every crumb of food, and the institution of a tight-fisted rationing program.

The next day we returned to our own flat, and as a few weeks passed life assumed something like normality. People went back to work. The diamond bourse reopened. The occupying troops insisted only that we follow every letter of their regulations. Each merchant had to submit a complete inventory of gold holdings, diamonds, and currency, and details of all transactions. The Germans wanted to be able to lay their hands on everything of value at a moment's notice.

The Nazis declared all organizations except their own illegal. Before their occupation, the Belgian Government had jailed the leaders of the Degrelle Belgian Nazi organization. Now these jackals returned with a great hue and cry to feed on the leavings of the lion. They tried to popularize Nazi ideology. They agitated far and wide, greeting the Germans as the saviors of Belgium who were about to liberate all Europe from bolshevism. The Nazis graciously freed most of the Belgian-Flemish prisoners-of-war and permitted them to return home. The Walloons, however, a more solidly anti-Nazi group, remained in prison until their final liberation by the Allies.

Not many weeks passed before Belgian and foreign democrats and left-wingers began to organize. First they attempted to counter Nazi propaganda. We Hungarians, too, gathered again, meeting in apartments in great secrecy, and decided to aid the Belgian movement against the invaders.

Our first action was to organize an illegal Hungarian paper, mimeographed on one sheet. We based the paper on English radio reports to which we listened despite the law prohibiting it. Once we were engaged in the active illegal fight we were all happier.

The movement grew. The unfolding of the inhuman policies of the Nazis drove the most disparate elements together in the Resistance. In December, 1940, the Nazis removed the mask of man with which they disguised the face of the jackal. As though it were simply an administrative move, they summoned all Jews to a special registration.

(The term "Jew," of course, included those with one Jewish grandparent.)

Then we made our first tragic error. We reported. Among us were many from Belgium and Holland who few realized were Jewish. Their forebears had lived in these countries for centuries, in a democratic atmosphere in which people concerned themselves little with the religious persuasion of their neighbors. Had they not registered they might have been alive today.

We went. We declared our ages, the age and sex of each member of the family, addresses, financial status. We were preparing a will and making our executioners the beneficiaries. We were handing them our children, our aged parents. We were aiding them in exterminating us.

Included in the statistics they demanded was the location of our gold teeth since these were systematically reclaimed from corpses.

Many of us realized our mistake almost as soon as we had finished registering. In a month's time a new order appeared: every Jewish business had to carry an identifying sign on the door. The anti-Jewish boycott was in effect. Gentile Belgians did not like this policy but they placed themselves in danger if they violated it. They dared call a Jewish family physician only in secret. The Walloons especially had nothing but contempt for the tactics of the Nazis and they undermined the program whenever they could.

Like all peoples, the people of Belgium had their Judases. Walloons and Flemings, a contemptible but vicious minority, went into the business of spying on their fellows. In return they received small privileges, and they groveled like dogs at the foot of the butcher's table.

Early in 1941 the Germans put every factory and shop on a war footing. All of Belgium's plant facilities worked for Hitler. Belgian workers had to accept employment or they received such miserable rations that they were certain to die of hunger. Yet these developments put the Resistance in a position to begin acts of sabotage. Members of the Resistance found jobs easily. The Nazis needed workers and they could not afford the luxury of being finicky about whom they hired.

Soon sabotage reached such proportions that products regularly emerged faulty from the factories, machines broke down, curious technical obstacles held up work. The Nazis were forced to recognize organized sabotage in every industry.

In February I took Henri to live with a family in Brussels because I had decided, together with a few others, to take employment in France. I am a carpenter by trade. The job was the construction of German hangars for an airport near the industrial city Lille. Our task was to fit roofs to the hangars.

The roofs were made in Belgium, but the Resistance worked well. Parts intended for Lille were misdirected to other destinations, and parts intended for different construction projects came to us at Lille.

This planned mismanagement delayed the work at least seven months. But the Germans soon caught on and when things got too warm we few Belgians and Hungarians gathered our belongings and returned to Brussels.

The decision to return was a decisive one. This was already September, 1941. To leave a job without permission was illegal. From that time onward my very life was illegal. I could no longer report my address to the police, according to regulations, or apply for food tickets. The brutal anti-Jewish edicts, growing ever more severe, made matters extremely difficult for me. By now I was wearing the compulsory Jewish-star badge.

The curfew for Jews was seven o'clock. Those on the streets after seven simply disappeared.

I had to learn how to stay alive.

4

March, 1942: the Germans sent a summons commanding all Jews in Antwerp between the ages of sixteen and twenty-two to report immediately at local Nazi offices, bringing a three-day supply of food and a change of clothing. The conqueror needed labor power in occupied France. Parents were warned that they, too, would be deported if they encouraged their children to disobey the order.

The Nazis promised the children easy work and good pay. The order netted them sixteen thousand Antwerp boys and girls. Then they extended the decree to all of Belgium.

Only a few months after this first deportation order, another followed. This time the German machine called for all men from the ages of twenty-two to forty. But now the Resistance took a hand on the basis of past experience and issued a manifesto, calling upon the Jewish people to disobey the order. At first many were afraid to take our advice, but they gradually realized that obedience meant death. The only hope of survival lay in resistance.

This manifesto created a tremendous organizational task for the Underground. Those who did not report had to live in hiding. We who were now leading the Underground had to supply them and their families with food or food tickets.

Food, even for those living legally, grew scarcer.

The Belgians became more dissatisfied, particularly when they saw the National Socialist Flemish, who were hand-in-glove with the invaders, receiving double rations and living high while the rest of the people were half starved. Consequently the Resistance grew and fought more boldly on two fronts: against the invader, and against native traitors.

In Antwerp Flemish collaborationists had taken control of the city administration. In Brussels, however, the Walloons had held on to most of the city offices. In almost all Brussels city departments there were decent officials, and we knew friend from foe.

For this reason we took most of those who disobeyed the deportation order to the vicinity of Brussels where we could still find homes for them and even register them at appropriate city bureaus.

By the summer of 1942 the Resistance was moving ahead with great energy. Every oppressive measure of the Nazis filled our ranks. The Germans discovered that there were Belgians who were hiding Jews. Rexist informers did their work. The Germans then decreed that if the Jews did not present themselves for deportation they would take young Belgians and send them to Germany rather than France. Then the Germans began seizing people on the streets. Those who could not prove they were working were sent to concentration camps, to forced labor, or to extermination camps.

It was dangerous for any young person or middle-aged man to appear on the streets. Degrelle, Belgium's quisling (who now enjoys the hospitality of his fellow-jackal, Franco), was strutting about Brussels in his elegant SS uniform. The Nazis exhorted the youth to join the SS and help "exterminate bolshevism." Some, who were Nazi or Rexist sympathizers, joined. Others volunteered to escape starvation. All of these became cannon fodder on the Eastern Front, and the promise the Nazis made to give their families double-rations was soon honored in the breach.

In the fall of 1942 the Resistance organized military groups in every Belgian city. We answered terror with terror. We dressed as civilians, but acted under Army discipline. We blew up a German military store-house. We demolished a Nazi movie theater filled with seven hundred and fifty German soldiers enjoying a Hitler film.

Following the explosion of the movie theater the Germans began the savage practice of taking hostages. It was then that the Walloon Mayor of Brussels proved himself a true hero. He issued a declaration to the people, calling upon them to sabotage German decrees and defy the oppressor. He then submitted his resignation and awaited his arrest, which came the following day. But the declaration had a powerful effect. German troop trains were blown up or derailed. Railway bridges disappeared at night. Fires broke out. The broad Belgian Resistance absorbed the foreign-speaking Underground groups, and the "Independence Front" appeared under a unified leadership.

The Belgian Resistance was now an Army.

5

Etta Kostelnik was a little past thirty, her face somewhat hard, but her eyes clear, kind, filled with the pain of much bitter struggle. She wore a shabby dress. There were gray threads in her black hair.

By day she worked, washing, ironing, housecleaning in the city of Brussels where she lived with her twelve-year-old son in one room on the Rue de Rivage. None of us knew how this wife of a Hungarian Catholic worker came to be in Belgium, nor did we ask, although we had heard that Franco's mercenaries had murdered her husband during the invasion of Spain.

Etta was high in the ranks of the heroines of the Resistance. In Catholic Belgium a Catholic working woman could live a comparatively peaceful life with her family, especially when that family was only one small boy. Etta, however, rejected such a peaceful life. Driven by concern for her Hungarian anti-Nazi countrymen, and for the Jewish people, she entered the Resistance.

As the least likely among us to be suspect, Etta had the job of keeping our most incriminating documents in her apartment, as well as the hand-mimeograph machine with which we published our illegal Hungarian paper. She also distributed the paper to its readers, every one of whose names and addresses she hid in her home. She also managed the money and food tickets which the Resistance supplied to those in need of them. (Armed partisans stole these tickets from the distribution center, or received them from patriotic Belgian authorities who were helping those in hiding.)

Etta Kostelnik's hands were full enough. During her working day, and at night when her work was done, she came and went tirelessly, particularly to more public places where better known people could not show themselves without risking their lives. Her little boy was her faithful assistant. He worked in the same spirit as his mother. He delivered papers, took relief to people in hiding, carried messages, and bore the responsibility for hundreds of lives—all with the tragic seriousness and dignity that a child may sometimes attain.

One day Stephen Molnar, leader of the Hungarian partisans in Belgium, rushed into my place. Sparing his words, he asked whether Etta's son knew my address or anything else about me.

Etta's son? I must have stared at him because he felt his question required explanation. I replied that the boy knew nothing about me since my name was not on Etta's lists.

Stephen Molnar threw himself down on the sofa like one who wishes to extort from life a moment's peace and quiet. Then he gave me the facts. "The Gestapo have Etta's boy. They're probably beating him. They may get something out of him."

"What happened?"

"Someone betrayed Etta!" Someone betrayed Etta! Someone sold his dignity and his right to life for the lying promise of a "double-ration!"

Molnar continued. "Three Gestapo men went to her flat about five o'clock this afternoon. She usually gets home then, but only the boy was there. They took him and they must be grilling him now. I notified all the others. I left you to the last."

"How did you get to know all this?" I asked. He hesitated. Then he said, quietly, "I was there when it happened."

I stared blankly. Molnar had a reputation for getting out of tight spots, but his statement surprised me nevertheless.

"I got away," he explained. "The neighbors warned Etta when she got near the house. Friends are taking her to the French border now." He rose, stretched, and took his hat. "I'll have to hurry. I've got a lot to do."

Molnar stopped short in the doorway, drew his revolver from his hip pocket, and examined it. Four of the chambers were empty. He took four fresh cartridges from a box and reloaded the weapon. Then he left without another word.

Days later I heard the story of the four empty chambers. Molnar never bragged. He never talked much, for that matter. Evidently the secret police, having found no sign of Etta, began to bully her boy.

The boy said he knew nothing. Then the Gestapo men searched every inch of the apartment. They found the lists of names, the illegal mimeo machine, the forged identification papers, addresses of fugitive Jews, and names of people who contributed money.

One of the Brownshirts went to the entrance of the house to prevent anyone from warning Etta. The others stayed in the flat, studying the papers, and slapping the boy around. It was then that Stephen Molnar arrived. He thought Etta would be at home, and he was carrying material for her Underground work. Since the Brownshirt at the door was in civilian clothes, Molnar paid no attention to him. He pressed Etta's bell and started toward the stairs. The Nazi moved over to him quickly and pressed his gun into Molnar's back.

"What's your business with that woman?"

"Nothing important. She does housework for us.

I want to tell her not to come tomorrow because we won't be home."

"You can talk about it upstairs." The Gestapo man nudged Molnar with the gun.

Molnar walked up obediently, with raised arms, but when they reached the top step, he suddenly gave a violent kick backward. His foot landed full in the German's belly. The German rolled and somersaulted down the stairs, but long before, he reached the landing Molnar had fired twice at his moving target. The Gestapo man had dropped his gun. Molnar raced for it. He knew that others would immediately rush out to investigate the shots. He took cover behind a pillar in the ground floor hall.

Two Germans appeared on the stairs. Molnar fired one shot at each. (We later discovered he wounded both.) Then he hurried away through the gathering crowd of neighbors.

Stephen Molnar notified everyone on Etta's lists in time for them to make good their escape.

That night Belgian and Hungarian partisans took Etta across the French border where she immediately joined the French Resistance. Under pressure from a Hungarian Catholic Mission the Nazis released her son. He had not broken under their beatings. Months after the liberation of Paris, Etta herself surrendered her arms as a Marquis soldier. She now wears a row of decorations on her blouse. Splendid as they are, these decorations cannot pay sufficient homage to a woman who was flesh, blood, and spirit of the fighting anti-fascist.

6

Germans killed children. This fact violates every concept we have of human beings. Not only did Nazis kill children, but the most repulsive aspect of their bestiality was their emphasis on the method and "science" of this murder. At one period during the war a half million Gestapo heroes busied themselves with tearing children from their parents and then suffocating them in gas chambers.

It began in 1942. We were well aware of the German "order of attack" against the civilian world.

First the left-wing of the working class (with a very supple definition of "left-wing"); then the Jews, particularly Jewish mothers and children. After that, the world, in some kind of order conceived by maniacal brains. Today we know that only fifteen per cent of the Hungarian Jews returned to Hungary after the victory of the Allies.

There was scarcely a child among them. We know that mothers of small children were the first to reach the gas chambers—and their children with them.

What makes this so incomprehensible to the civilized mind, which is ordinarily wary of "war atrocity stories," is the attempt to find some rhyme or reason in such a policy. It is difficult to accept such depravity as real, particularly when this very depravity helped mobilize the world against fascism.

During the time I did forced labor in France, or lived in illegality in Belgium, I had placed Henri in the care of various Jewish families. (I was divorced from Henri's mother and she had remarried.) Then the situation in Antwerp became unbearable. Flemish collaborationists were delivering Jews by the thousands to the Nazis. I moved on to Brussels. Toward the end of 1942 the position of Jews in Brussels grew almost as dangerous as in Antwerp.

Every two or three months I had to find another refuge for Henri since his protectors often fell into Nazi hands. Finally the situation was such that it was no longer safe to place him with a Jewish family. The Nazis were now raiding houses and taking both the children and the adults who sheltered them.

Since the children could not do useful work the Nazis murdered them. The same applied to adults who were unfit for beastlike labor. Auschwitz, the Polish death camp, was an ample host.

Finally I found a place for Henri with a Christian Walloon family who knew the situation and willingly offered to feed and protect him. But the Nazis were determined to shut this door, too. They soon discovered that Christian families were harboring Jewish children under false names. They decreed that Christians guilty of sheltering Jewish children would be subject to the same laws as those affecting the Jews.

When the decree appeared in the papers I went to the family that was caring for Henri, and told them I did not wish them to take such a frightful risk. The head of the family advised me to speak to the Abbe Edouard Froidure, a Catholic priest in charge of a children's camp.

The next day I called on the priest. I discovered that he knew my way of life, my illegal position, and my activities with the Resistance, but without any hesitation he received my son at the camp, gave him another name, and prepared a false birth certificate for him. He refused to take any money from me.

In the camp were some hundred children from the ages of five to twelve. Some looked Jewish to me, but the Abbe said nothing and I knew better than to be curious. Every Sunday I visited Henri, bringing a little package of whatever comforts I could get together with the help of friends in the Resistance. Henri was happy there. The Abbe was good to the children, and he saw to their schooling as well. Henri was permitted this little luxury of comfort and safety for four whole months.

Then some traitor reported to the Nazis that the Abbe was concealing Jewish children in the camp. Three SS men appeared at the cloister. (They always traveled in threes for protection against non-master races.) "We are told you're hiding Jewish children, monsieur l'Abbe," said their spokesman.

The Abbe held his ground. "No, monsieur, that's a mistake. There are no Jewish children here." He produced birth-certificates, genuine and forged, identifying every child. He was self-assured, calm, without fear. But the SS troops were not easily deceived. They ordered the Abbe to assemble all the children and line them up. The chief of the SS men began to address them in kindly and gentle tones.

"Children," he said, "I want to ask you a few questions. Now I'm going to give some candy to everybody who gives me the correct answers. Pay close attention. How many of you know how to speak French? Raise your hands!"

Every child immediately raised his hand. The Abbe knew what was to follow, but he did not lose his self-possession. The Nazi spoke again.

"Very good. Now how many can speak Flemish? Raise your hands!"

Again every hand went up.

"Splendid! Now how many can speak German? Raise your hands!"

A few small children who knew German and wanted candy, raised their hands. Then came the fourth question.

"Now how many of you can speak Jewish? Raise your hands!"

Three of the younger children raised their hands. They were proud of themselves, all smiles. They knew all four languages. Evidently they would get the candy. My son was not among the three. He did not know how to speak Yiddish, but even if he had, he was by this time old and wise enough to have kept his silence.

The SS chief turned to the priest. "Well, monsieur l'Abbe, what do you say to this?" The Nazis ordered the three children to step forward. They obeyed instantly, still expecting candy. The Nazis inspected them closely, and then departed.

They returned the following day to fetch the children and the priest. The children were no longer there but the Abbe was still at his post. In Gestapo headquarters he was brutally beaten for two weeks, but he refused to tell where the children were. I later discovered that the Abbe, together with a number of other priests, was connected with the Resistance. The others had hidden the children away. The Germans placed the Abbe Froidure in an internment camp where he remained until the Allies freed him. The Nazis could never force him to ignore the injunction, "Suffer little children to come unto Me."

7

On Saturday, November 6, 1943, I dressed, slipped a list of names into my pocket, and prepared to deliver identification papers, forged certificates, and food coupons to a list of Underground fighters. I was then working for a woman named Madame Stephan whose husband, a Christian Hungarian, had been sentenced to hard labor for life for "activities inimical to the State." Madame Stephan helped us in every possible way, and although the Gestapo kept constant watch, they were never able to collect evidence against her.

Madame Stephan owned a furniture shop. On that day—as on all Saturdays—my job was to see that furniture was properly loaded on the van, and to assist in deliveries, work which I could usually complete in an hour's time. Since the truck was setting out in the direction of many people on my list, I climbed aboard and stood beside the furniture in the back while Madame Stephan and the driver rode in the cab. As the truck turned into the Avenue Louis I noticed a Gestapo car behind us. Since the main headquarters of the Gestapo were in the Avenue Louis, this did not disturb me at first, but when we left the main thoroughfare and the car still followed, I began to feel nervous. Five minutes later the car passed us and I recognized in it one of the most notorious of stool-pigeons: Monsieur Jacques who specialized in delivering Jews to the Nazis. Monsieur was staring at me as his car passed. The sight of him was enough. Squeezing against the side of the truck, I immediately pushed all the papers I was carrying, with the exception of my identification certificate, between the sideboards and the canvas covering. When the truck slowed down for a turn, I jumped off and hurried to a newsstand a few yards away. There I asked for a paper and fumbled in my pockets for a coin, trying to look like a casual citizen. Before I found the coin three men were at my side. They didn't say a word. They hustled me into their car and began searching me, but all they found were the false identification papers in my inside pocket. One of the men remarked, "We should have stopped the truck." Another hit me in the face and asked, "What did you leave in the truck?" Before I could answer the third man hit me on the ear.

Evidently they were dividing the fun among them. "Whose truck was it?" they demanded.

"I don't know. I climbed up on it because it was going my way."

"Where were you going, Jew?"

"Nowhere. I just wanted to get to the end of town and take a walk." This was such an obvious lie that it earned me a smashing blow full in the face. "Why did you jump off?"

"I saw the police car. I wanted to get away because I'm a Jew."

They examined my papers again. The address was correct although the Jewish stamp was missing. The Gestapo men decided to take me to my home, hoping to find others there, family or friends. As we rode along they continued their questions. "Where did you get these false papers?" I didn't answer. They beat me up again but to my surprise, they didn't repeat the question. At my apartment they quickly found that

I lived there quite alone. Neighbors whom they questioned verified the fact.

The Gestapo men then searched the apartment thoroughly, and before they took me away they permitted me to gather a few personal belongings. Although they searched my place with exemplary efficiency, none of them had thought of taking down the license number of the truck. Madame Stephan was still safe. I had a long wait in Gestapo headquarters in the Avenue Louis where I was taken for further questioning.

At six that evening I was supposed to have kept an appointment with Nicholas Sapir, a Resistance member, who was to bring two women partisans to our meeting to discuss some organizational matters.

I was worried about Sapir. But my greatest anxiety was for my son. It was true that he was in a safe place where nuns were caring for him, but what would happen to him if the Nazis did away with me? What would he think if I never answered the letters which he wrote every week, addressing me by an assumed name and signing an assumed name of his own? I had arranged, of course, to have someone else write the boy in case I were arrested, and to send him packages from time to time, but this was little consolation as I sat in the waiting room of the Gestapo headquarters.

A harsh voice interrupted my melancholy thoughts, "Go inside!" Inside was where a man delivered himself to his enemies. First I had to submit to an interview in the course of which Nazi clerks recorded pertinent facts concerning myself. Then they put me into a basement room which already held about forty-five occupants, men, women, and children, all of whom were waiting for the group to become sufficiently large to be shipped away. Every adult there, without exception, bore the marks of blows.

Since I was the newcomer they immediately surrounded me and asked a thousand questions. They told me that when our number reached fifty we would go to Malin.

All of us in that basement room were the victims of Monsieur Jacques, the informer. At eleven o'clock the Nazis thrust two more men and a child into the room. We asked them the standard question. "Who betrayed you?"

"Monsieur Jacques, of course." Monsieur received a thousand francs for each betrayal (a better business man than Judas Iscariot!). I found it difficult to resign myself to my circumstances and surprised to see others take things so lightly.

In retrospect I think it was because we of the Resistance knew better than to avoid facts. The mood of many of the adults was quite cheerful. They even sang old Jewish songs. Since it happened to be a Saturday there was a Sabbath feeling among the more religious ones. Only the children were restless and excited.

At half past one the guard told us to get our things together. We were leaving at two o'clock for Malin, the assembly camp.' After a half hour had passed, two armed soldiers entered, counted us, led us to the yard, and ordered us to clamber aboard trucks.

They warned us that anyone attempting escape would be immediately shot. The trucks were open in back and as we sped through the city we said farewell to the familiar streets. Now and then one of us recognized a face. Occasionally a man or woman might wave at us and cry out, "Courage! It can't last much longer!"

Some of the women in the truck were weeping. We tried to cheer them up. We played with the children and reproached their mothers. Why had they kept their children at home instead of in hiding when they had known all along what to expect? Why? Why? The women all had the same answer: they preferred to be with their children when they met whatever fate awaited them.

This was certainly a natural attitude, but it was an attitude the Resistance was fighting to break down. A young woman's only chance of life was to be without children. A child's only chance of life was to be hidden away from its mother. But what a futile game it was to reproach the women as we sat on that truck on the way to Malin!

It took us only an hour to reach the assembly camp. At Malin they put us in a barrack. We saw only German soldiers—not a single prisoner. Later we found out that when new prisoners arrived nobody was allowed outside. Even to look out was verboten, and guards fired at any face appearing at a window. SS troopers, commanded by a Hamburg captain, herded us into an office where fifteen of the women and five of the men were assigned work.

A Nazi, toying with a many, ordered us to surrender our valuables. There would be a thorough search later, and he would flog those who attempted to conceal anything. We turned in our "valuables," papers, and photographs. Then Nazi clerical workers entered us on the accounts in two categories: favored and non-favored.

The favored category comprised Rumanian, Swiss, Spanish, and Hungarian Jews. These were differentiated from the others by the letter Z and a number. "Favored" meant that the prisoner would go not to Poland, but to Germany where there were no gas chambers. The "non-favored" group included Czech, Polish, German, Austrian, Belgian, Dutch, and French Jews.

These were given numbers but no letters. When our pockets were empty the Nazis took us, four by four, into a barren room where we faced two SS men from whose countenances every trace of the human had disappeared. One of them shouted, "Undress!"

We were shocked into a moment's paralysis. There were young women among us, children. The Nazi repeated the order once. We began to remove our clothes. A girl hesitated and the Nazi brought the whip down across her back. She cried out, perhaps not so much from pain as from humiliation and shock. Of course they might have segregated the men from the women before the search began, but such delicacy was evidently no part of Kultur. The two men in charge were obviously sexual perverts and it was easy to detect their ugly excitement as they searched the naked women, looking into their arm-pits and private parts, ostensibly after "diamonds." They took particular delight in removing the pad of a menstruating woman, examining it, and returning it to her.

While these two continued, others searched our clothes. They opened the seams, tore up the hems, and then gave us back the torn rags. Still others searched our parcels in the same fashion. When the ordeal was over, they hung numbers around our necks and led us to our quarters. I was assigned to a room that held sixty people. All of them rushed at me, demanding the names of those who had arrived in this shipment.

Every prisoner still had ties with someone on the "outside" whose freedom he cherished. It did not take me long to learn the situation at Malin. Transports leaving Malin were supposed to contain fourteen hundred people. Prisoners waited until that number assembled in the camp. At this time, however, there were only four hundred and twenty prisoners, including my group. Generally speaking, conditions in Malin were bearable. Thanks to the Jewish Committee of Belgian Relief we received food three times a day. Most of the prisoners did not have to work which made it possible to get along on the spare rations.

Yet employment was something to be envied at Malin. Those who received the few jobs in the offices, the carpenter shop, the kitchen, the tailor shop, were exempt from transport deportations. This made them extremely watchful of their "jobs." If they committed the slightest irregularity they were listed in the next transport.

Some of those whom I met had been so cautious that they had succeeded in holding their jobs for two years. With the exception of the hours between seven and eight, morning and evening, when we were lined up for a "walk" in the courtyard, we spent our time in the barracks. The families slept in groups, side by side, on sacks filled with straw.

Single people lay wherever there was room, men and women mingling in enforced intimacy that soon enough became commonplace. Every day we chose a new squad of two men and two women to clean the quarters as best they could. Only the men emptied the slops and this task, too, we organized on a democratic basis, the college professor sharing duties with the Jewish old-clothes man.

Here at Malin there was ample evidence that wherever there are people, there are Etta Kostelniks. Anya was such a person. I met her the first evening during the compulsory walk in the courtyard. She was a Hungarian woman named Madame Simon whom all the prisoners called Anya (little mother) because of her bravery and unselfish conduct. Anya had been a year in Malin. She worked in the tailor shop, and being an "employee," she was exempt from deportation. Her two children, a girl of eighteen and a boy of twenty, had been Resistance fighters, but the Gestapo had caught them and exterminated them in Auschwitz.

The Germans did not know that Anya was their mother. The selfish caution of the other job-holders was not for Anya. She was always willing to risk her position to help other less fortunate prisoners, although her life was at stake. She sent and received messages. She gave away whatever little extra scraps of food she could collect. Anya told me that the Nazis had caught her daughter only two weeks before she herself was arrested.

The girl had remained in Malin a few days before she was transported to Auschwitz. Anya's son was caught in 1941 and sentenced to two years in prison for "political activity." The Belgian prison commander had taken a liking to the boy and helped him escape. The young man rejoined the Resistance. I myself had met him several times on the "outside," and like everyone else, grew fond of him. One day he disappeared. We knew he must have been taken to Malin. Anya told me that when he arrived she did not dare betray the relationship between them.

Silently, and with no show of emotion, she shook hands with him as though she were being introduced. Not long afterward she saw him leave for Auschwitz.

Since the death of her children, Anya's first concern was the welfare of those youngsters who came to Malin without their parents. Anya protected them, fed them, and sewed for them. Anya saw them through. She worked in her tailor shop, risking her life anew every day, while the months dragged on and twenty-one transports, each filled with fourteen hundred prisoners, left the camp. The departure of every transport meant the death of more of Anya's children.

The majority of the prisoners were fairly calm although we all knew that these relatively pleasant days were only an interlude before the grim life of some concentration camp. We tried not to think of the future. We could put our time to the best use by preparing ourselves, physically and morally, for whatever was to come. In my group were six Hungarians and I found among them that same Nicholas Sapir with whom I had the appointment the day of my arrest. Like everyone in the camp, we awaited the arrival of "new ones." The "new ones" brought news. Some brought us hope as well because they said that the Russians were at the Polish border and still advancing. Inevitably "new ones" included friends, relatives.

Anya's younger sister arrived with one contingent. A woman from Antwerp saw her two children reach the camp. Aladar Rosner, a Hungarian partisan who had fought in Spain with the International Brigade for three years, was among the "new ones." 'He brought word of Stephen Molnar's activities, and told us that Nazi guards now patrolled the streets in threes rather than in pairs. That was a victory for the Resistance since it meant we were immobilizing more Nazi .soldiers. Monsieur Jacques and his fellows worked hard.

Our numbers grew. Hungarian Jews, many betrayed by their Consulate, came by the dozens. After my third week there we were six hundred all told. Another eight hundred and we would be ready for deportation. We counted days, calculated probabilities, speculated on our possible destination, and those of us who prayed, prayed that it would not be Auschwitz. We all knew that after Malin a man could have but one objective in life: survival.

8

The town of Malin has always lived in the legends of Western European Jews. It was to Malin that the Inquisitors brought Jews who refused to be converted, to be burned at the stake.

In our barrack in Malin was a group of about thirty Turkish Jews. Actually they were Spanish Jews whose ancestors had fled the Inquisition and the threat of Malin to take refuge in Turkey. Like many Sephardic Jews they still retained Spanish as their language, not the modern Spanish but the Golden Age Spanish of the days of Cervantes. Many of them who had been in Belgium thirty years or more, spoke French and Flemish as well.

And now, after four centuries, they were repeating the bitter history of their ancestors. They were back in Malin. Yet there was a difference. Many of the Inquisitors had, at least, the conviction of religious fanaticism to justify their tortures, but nothing nobler than bestial sadism inspired Hitler's new Torquemada's.

The Turkish Jews were "favored." They wore the letter Z because the Turkish Government made some efforts to protect them. This group would often sit in a corner and sing the old Spanish-Jewish songs of their tradition, sorrowful, plaintive tunes reflecting centuries of suffering. We felt as though they were extemporaneous songs, composed on the moment's inspiration, because they expressed our mood so well. Doubtless the songs had that same extemporaneous quality four centuries ago when in the corner of some dungeon groups of Spanish Jews awaited the stake as we awaited the concentration camp.

Strangely enough we felt a special sorrow for the Turkish Jews as though their fate was somehow worse than ours. But soon afterward there was only one person whose fate concerned us, and that person was Anya.

A prisoner tried to escape by climbing down a rope from a window. He scrambled down the wall—and landed in the arms of a guard. The Nazis beat him half to death, put him in solitary confinement, and starved him. They also decreed that the rest of us would be denied the right to receive packages or food from the outside.

We were learning. We learned, for instance, that the attempt to escape was nothing but tragic folly.

Escape was a tactic for the outside world, not for the world of Malin. Following this attempt new regulations directed against us made it almost impossible to deliver an important message to our friends in Brussels. Anya heard of this and she undertook to do the job.

There was a tailor in the tailor shop whose "official job" exempted him and his family from the deportation lists. He had lived at the camp with his family, in reasonable comfort, for fifteen months. He was mean, hard. He never did a prisoner the slightest service, even when there was little risk. His only concern was himself and his family. Anya discovered that he was going to send thread into the city to be exchanged for thread of another color. She asked him to conceal a note in the thread, but he refused. That night Anya found the spool, unwound the thread, wrapped the message around the reel, and re-wound it.

The next day the tailor, who had the privilege of receiving visitors, gave the thread to a friend. One of the soldiers on guard became suspicious. He unwound the thread and discovered the letter. The officials immediately degraded (or raised) the tailor to the rank of common prisoner, together with his family. He protested, declared himself innocent, but it did him no good. The Nazis ordered him into the next transport with his wife and children. This order could mean only one thing: Auschwitz and the gas chambers.

Anya could not bear this. She reported at once to the commandant and confessed. In that confession was another lesson to guide the work of prisoners. It was a futile gesture because the commandant, after having Anya flogged and removed from work where she could be helpful to us, refused to cancel the orders deporting the tailor and his family.

Poor Anya spent days weeping over the outcome of her attempt to help us. We could not console her. She was unable to forget the tailor's two children and she felt that their blood was on her hands. For day's she remained in her room because she did not want to come face to face with the tailor.

We who had written and signed the note were also called into the office for questioning. Luckily the man who had translated the letter from Hungarian to German covered us so cleverly that we were able to pass it off without much trouble.

Anya wept. The tailor trembled. We waited. Five weeks had passed since our arrival, and there were still only seven hundred prisoners in Malin. We thought that we would remain there another five or six weeks, after which the "favored" would go to Germany, the "unfavored" to Auschwitz.

9

When we were walking in the courtyard two days later a group of soldiers suddenly appeared and ordered us back to the barracks. We thought that a new shipment of prisoners was arriving because we were not allowed out at such times. We were mistaken. The German commandant appeared a few minutes later to inform us that all male prisoners over fifteen years of age must pack and gather at the main office to await deportation. He added that the women would follow in two days, a bit of information designed to give false comfort to those of us who were with their wives and children.

In previous transports men, women, and children had left together. The sudden tragedy of this separation, therefore, was totally unexpected. The women wept. Some became hysterical. Mothers of young sons felt they would never see them again. Wives bid farewell to their husbands, knowing that it was a final farewell. Young men and girls, who had first met here in Malin in the most helpless of conditions, left each other like lovers of long standing. Then the women helped us pack. Anya was busy tying bundles for six men, and trying to cheer the others meanwhile. Everyone said, "We'll meet again."

Nobody believed it. While we were preparing our departure a Nazi guard intruded to make sure that no one wrote notes that could be thrown from the trucks when we left.

There were sixty-nine men and boys in our transport, the smallest group that had ever left Malin. Among us were twenty-three Hungarians including Stephen Precz who had been a member of a band of several hundred prisoners who had escaped under the leadership of Stephen Molnar. He had been arrested again, beaten and tormented for six months, and finally sent to Malin. Like all men who had once escaped, he wore a red ribbon tied around his arm and his head was shaven. The Nazis had murdered his father, mother, and three brothers in Antwerp. Only he and his five-year-old son remained of the Precz family.

Our farewells did not last long. SS men pulled us apart and hustled us along to the office. We were all intensely disturbed. The unexpected order, the excitement of saying good-by, our feeling that this small transport must have some sinister purpose, overwhelmed us. Suddenly an SS trooper stood before me, shouted something I didn't understand, and then struck me with all his strength. I staggered and the blood ran from my cut lips. Then I realized that I had forgotten to remove my hat when I entered the office.

Among our group was an old Turkish Jew who had been in the infirmary for days, suffering from pneumonia. Two soldiers held him under the arms and dragged him along because he didn't have the strength to walk. The old man was shaking with fever when they wrapped him in a blanket. We were upset by his presence among us, by his obviously serious condition—and by the further thought that if he was in our transport there seemed little likelihood that we would go to a work camp. If we did not go to a work camp, where else but Auschwitz?

Soldiers searched us. They confiscated every pencil and scrap of paper to keep us from writing notes. Then we submitted personal information about ourselves once more, clerks recorded it, and we marched to small trucks. Since there were only two trucks for all of us we were packed in so tightly that we could hardly breathe. We had no idea where we were being taken but we knew that if we had to travel the entire way under those conditions, none of us would be alive on arrival.

Just before we set off the commandant addressed us. "Tomorrow morning you will go to Germany. Since you are citizens of our allies, you will not be taken to Poland. You are going to a prisoner-of-war camp where we also detain English prisoners-of-war.

You have nothing to fear. No one will harm you. When the war ends we will set you free."

Perhaps the commandant was trying to be human. Perhaps he actually wanted to bolster our morale. Certainly he felt that the end of the war meant the victory of Germany, but we who knew it would mean the defeat of Germany felt certain that when defeat was imminent the Nazis would try to butcher us to the last man.

The commandant also told us that we were to spend the night in Brussels, a welcome bit of news since Brussels was only an hour's ride and we could survive that hour's standing—thirty-five men in a truck designed to hold, at best, ten. We were so close to one another that our arms were pinned to our sides, and we could neither wipe the sweat from our faces or blow our noses, yet the commandant—perhaps moved by some grisly humor—concluded by reminding us that guards would shoot down anyone attempting escape. He also hinted that we had better keep in mind the welfare of relatives left in Malin, implying that they, too, would pay for any misconduct on our part.

The commandant did not have a trusting audience for his speech. Other transports, containing "citizens of our allies," had ended up at Auschwitz despite all promises, or at Buchenwald where the Nazis killed prisoners by overwork and starvation instead of by gas.

After an hour of stifling travel we arrived in Brussels but we saw nothing of the city, partly because it was dark, and partly because we could not turn to look. The trucks finally stopped in the courtyard of Gestapo headquarters. We literally fell out because our limbs were numb and we could not stand at first. When we eventually got to our feet we saw that six armed soldiers and two motorcycle troopers with mounted machine guns accompanied each truck.

The guards lined us up for the inevitable count. It did not take long but it froze our blood and for a moment we could not move. We had started with sixty-nine men. The count showed sixty-eight. Once again the Nazis counted. Still sixty-eight. I looked around for Precz who had no family about whom to worry. I could not see him. Sapir was standing near me. "What do you think?" I whispered. "Who got away?"

"I don't see Precz," he said. He was thinking the same thoughts as myself, yet it seemed unbelievable that anyone could have made his way through the tightly-packed men in the truck, and then through a gauntlet of armed guards and motorcyclists.

Another roll-call, loud shouts, the snapping of whips. We were not the only frightened men. The Nazi escort was frightened, too, because they would get off little better than we if a prisoner had escaped.

Finally someone looked inside the truck. There was the sixty-ninth prisoner. It was the old Turkish Jew with pneumonia who lay dead on the floor. No one could tell how long he had been standing, packed in among the others, but mercifully dead. The guards took us to the basement where they assigned us tiny cells—ten to a cell. It was impossible to lie down. Sitting was as much as we could manage. The guard told us that we would be on our way by eight in the morning. He said our destination was Germany and even declared that we would have the fantastic luxury of riding in a regular railway coach!

To those interested in fascist schedules, let me confirm that the trains in Nazi Germany ran on time—to Auschwitz, to Buchenwald, to Marienbad.

At seven the next morning the guard awoke those of us who were cat-napping. SS men jammed us into the same two trucks, but this time we only traveled a few kilometers to the Gare du Nord. The train was waiting, German soldiers filled the station, and the few civilians who traveled by grace of special passes were collaborators, spies, and Resists.

We were amazed when the guards assigned us comfortable accommodations, eight to a compartment. It was even possible to sleep, sitting up, of course. The officer in charge of the train visited us and made courteous inquiries about our food. He insisted that we would receive good treatment. After all, didn't he personally forbid the soldiers to cause U£ any discomfort? If we had any complaint he urged us to lay it directly before him.

We had never met such an SS officer before. It must have been a hallucination. There was something, I was sure, that lay beneath his curious conduct. My instinct warned me not to trust him, but nevertheless his courtesy raised our spirits a little.

When we asked him our destination he said he had not been told. He knew only that we would go to a proper internment camp where we would be treated like prisoners-of-war. He smiled when he said it, and his smile was charming.

We had a thousand unanswered questions. If they were really taking us to a decent internment camp, why had the women and children been left behind? We speculated. One prisoner suggested, "Maybe our job will be to build a new camp. Maybe the women will come when we're finished."

Another applied human standards to his captors.

"There aren't enough trains available. They don't want to pack us in the way they've been doing before this."

Precz, however, was not given to self-deception. He told us he intended to escape. He was not impressed by the rosy picture of an internment camp with its English prisoners. If they were taking us to our death, he preferred to be shot while escaping rather than to go sheep-like into a gas chamber. The rest of us dissuaded him.

We were only sixty-eight, but we reminded him that we had left behind in Malin one hundred and thirty-five members of our families.

When we crossed the border into Germany we soon saw that life there was livelier, traffic more heavy. Precz realized that escape had become impractical. Around us were signs of the war: the rubble of bombed-out railway stations, city streets in ashes, houses reduced to dust. Bombs had torn off the flesh of Cologne, leaving only the battered skeleton of a city. The commandant pointed out the window. "You people complain!" he said. "You say we mistreat you! But look what your friends have done to us. Their bombs kill our women and children every night. But at worst we force you to work!" Did he have a conscience that he felt impelled to defend himself? We didn't ask who had begun the holocaust. We didn't inquire about Auschwitz and the gas chambers. We said nothing of Coventry and Warsaw. We didn't tell him that we had neither time nor inclination to weep for his women and children, to mourn his Cologne.

We stayed three hours in that wreck of a city. At nine that evening, the train moved out through the special darkness of the blackout. From far off we heard the muffled scream of a siren, the faint hum of airplane motors. Quiet overlay our thoughts. We fell asleep while the train bore us relentlessly on toward that unknown of which we knew too much.

10

The next day was December 15, 1943. That was the day when our speculations ended.

A prisoner who had traveled in Germany recognized the landscape. "We're in Thuringia," he said in a dead voice. "We're coming near Weimar."

No one answered. We looked at one another, and we saw in each other's faces the same silent dread. There was only one camp near Weimar, and that was Buchenwald. Buchenwald. No gas chambers in Buchenwald, but having said that you were left with nothing else to say. In Buchenwald there were only males over the age of fourteen. In Buchenwald the Nazis forced prisoners into the most brutal and hideous possible existence. In Buchenwald hundreds of men died every day in the week from two diseases: overwork and starvation. In Buchenwald you found fascism without frills.

Buchenwald discipline was famous for being so intolerable that few could bear up under it for long. Originally it had been a camp for "politicals." It was still that, but the concept of politics was now broader. The Nazis now numbered among political enemies all Jews, trade unionists, liberals, leftists, democrats, professors who would not betray their calling to teach an ersatz science, or children who repeated anti-Nazi jokes even if they were too young to understand them.

Our humane commandant himself changed now that we were near Buchenwald. He had been having his fun. He no longer spoke sweetly. The smile, once charming, was now the familiar smile of the sadist. He enjoyed our reactions with the same lustful pleasure I have seen on the faces of so many Nazis in the proximity of torture.

It was difficult for us to look Precz in the face.

What damn fools we had been to talk him out of escaping! But Precz did not accuse. He joined us as we tried to cheer the more faint-hearted among us, telling them what was so very true: our only weapon was hope. If we surrendered that, we were surely lost.

We helped the children and the more apathetic men pack their belongings, and as we did, a curious pattern emerged, a pattern that I saw throughout Buchenwald and which was evident in all our activities. Those of us who had fought in the Resistance or had in our background some experience in organization, either in the trade union movement or in the political field, were the ones who did not surrender to apathy. The others, who had no such experience, who said, "What's the use?" who never learned to fight unitedly, looked with blank eyes at their surroundings and only muttered their thanks as we helped them. They had not yet learned what we knew: survival in Nazi Germany could only be a social achievement, and not an individual accident. They were candidates for death.

We reached Weimar at eleven in the morning and we found the station untouched by bombs. Over the city of Goethe and Wagner hung the heavy air of Buchenwald.

Whenever we faced some new horror, a fascist would demand that we stand up to be counted. We went through this customary procedure in the Weimar station. The count ended all hypocrisy.

There were no more smiles, no more assurances. Guards pushed us into convict vans equipped with individual cells. The cells were built to hold one person, but of course the Nazis put two in each so that we could not move behind the locked door.

When the painful forty-five-minute ride came to an end, they opened the doors of the trucks. Bitter cold winter winds struck our faces. We looked around the barren yard. Before us was a wide gate which bore the dreadful legend: konzentrations lager Buchenwald.

We had arrived.

11

In ten brief years the German people, actively or by the consent of silence, reduced five centuries of their own civilization and culture to the level of a Buchenwald. Buchenwald was not an aberration.

It was the pure expression of fascist thinking carried to its logical conclusion. It was in perfect harmony with the Germany which created it.

My fellow-prisoners and I looked up into the visage of the new German Kultur as we waited before the huge gateway for our possessions to arrive. Before us were triple thicknesses of electrically charged wire which surrounded the entire camp.

On the other side of the wire, not far from us, we could see the prisoners, fleshless, phlegmatic, as they came and went among the hundreds of barracks. They paid no attention to us. Here the "new ones" evidently created no hopeful stir.

Each prisoner wore a striped convict uniform with a number on the jacket which was repeated on the pants—a depressing little novelty. I had a vision of myself in such a uniform, walking slowly toward the extermination depot where the only record of my death would be my number. There were other novelties to occupy us, such as the manner in which the prisoners wore their hair. Some, in American Indian style, had shaved heads except for a strip about two centimeters wide which ran over the middle of the skull from the brow to the nape of the neck. Others had hair growing on either side of the skull while the crown of the head was shaved to the scalp.

In some circumstances the prisoners might have been weird or even comical, but in Buchenwald the sight was another affirmation of the carefully nurtured sadism of the Nazis. The hair dress was used to differentiate the prisoners so that guards could tell their nationality at a glance. This also made escape more difficult.

I looked around me at others in my group. They, too, were watching, and they too showed on their faces the same dismay that I felt. Our possessions arrived and then we found ourselves marching through the dread gateway and waiting in the courtyard. Now it was the outside world which we saw through the electrically charged wires. We noticed that next to each prisoner's number was a letter that indicated his nationality—P for Polish, R for Russian, U for Hungarian. A prisoner marked with a P passed close by and without pausing, muttered quickly to us under his breath, asking for cigarettes or something to eat. We would have gladly obliged but SS troopers arrived at that moment and marched us toward one of the barracks. We carried the miserable little bundles that contained all we owned.

Our first stop was the Reception Hall. This was no basement room, no crowded cellar. Rather it was a vast and beautifully equipped hall flanked by bathrooms. The prisoner-attendants who worked in this department entered us on the books, and while this was going on we had a little time to look around and exchange a few words with them. They wore the standard convict garb but they appeared better nourished, healthier than those on the outside. But their attitude shocked us. They were indifferent, off-hand. They asked no questions. They exhibited no curiosity about the "outside." But they did offer a few brief words of advice. "If you have anything to eat," they said, "eat it now. They'll take it away from you in a little while anyway."

The food that we had in our bundles wouldn't keep a man alive very long, but we did as they suggested. Nervous as we were, our minds too occupied to bother with our stomachs, we began to eat mechanically, sharing our scraps with the prisoner-attendants who bustled around us.

A Hungarian-speaking Czech said, "You've got another hour. Eat and smoke till then. After that they'll take whatever's left." We gave him some bread, salami, and cheese, all the leftovers of the food packages we had received while in Malin. I realized then why the prisoners who worked in the Reception Hall looked better fed than the others.

Every day a thousand or more new prisoners arrived, and every day they shared their scraps with the Reception Hall staff. But I also learned that before a man won an assignment to the Reception Hall he had to pass at least three years in Buchenwald. Among the staff were Czechs and Germans who had been six to eight years in the camp.

Although the prisoners asked us no questions, they answered ours. They spoke without emotion. They gave us the facts without attempting to delude us.

We would have to work like animals to earn a starvation diet. The death rate averaged one hundred and fifty to two hundred prisoners every day, but new ones were always on hand to fill the gaps. There were deportations from Buchenwald to other labor camps, or to the extermination chambers in Auschwitz. The charged wire confined between twenty and twenty-five thousand prisoners.

Most terrible of all to me, as I waited in the Reception Hall, was the apathy of the attendants who had lost interest in the war, the outside world, their friends and relatives. They had only one thing to request of us, the "new ones." That was food. Working in a death factory which encompassed all the life they knew, the rest of the world no longer existed for these men. They had forgotten how to hope for freedom, having nothing left for which to hope except food.

SS soldiers stepped in. Immediately everyone fell silent. They ordered us to stand at table and empty our pockets and bundles. After that they told us to strip and place our clothes alongside our other possessions. Again they asked for "valuables." The Nazis worked efficiently. Their well-planned and rigid system had no defects unless inhumanity can be considered a defect. They entered each item in a ledger, carefully describing the most worthless piece of trash. Then they threw our clothing into sacks, one" sack for each prisoner, marked with a name and prison number.

Standing there naked, shivering in the poorly heated Reception Hall, we thought that we would now receive our prison uniforms. But we soon found out that the search was not over.

Fascist efficiency extended to the technique employed to search a naked man. Guards lined us up before an SS trooper who stood with a slender cane in one hand. He commanded us to spread our legs.

First he probed our armpits with the tip of the cane, then stirred it about our genitals (doubtless seeking those elusive diamonds or gold bullion). Then he probed each man's anus with the end of the cane, after which (and in just this order) he prodded inside our mouths and under the tongue.

He searched all sixty-eight of us, one by one, in this manner, using the same cane. It was not a part of Kultur to wash or clean the cane in any way. Yet we were lucky. We learned that at other times hundreds and even thousands of new arrivals went through this ordeal, all standing nude for hours in that hall. In our case we were finished in an hour.

Our guards now led us to another chamber, the Hair-Cutting Division where other prisoners, using electric clippers, shaved us. We were ordered to stand on little boxes while the barbers clipped all the hair from our bodies, including our genital hair and the hair under our armpits. Since we were still to spend weeks in quarantine they did not shave our heads Indian fashion. We were now more naked than we had ever been in our lives, and for some incomprehensible reason the barbers who shaved us were naked as well. When we looked at one another we presented so ludicrous a spectacle that we discovered it was still possible to laugh.

The barbers swept all the fallen hair neatly together and put it into a sack. The Nazis were a thrifty herd. They had an industrial use for everything.

When they were not thrusting befouled canes into our mouths, the Nazis were also scrupulously clean. They led us next to the bath. First they ordered us into an enormous tub filled with dubious brackish water. We had to sit down in this water and duck under several times so that every part of us should be covered by the disgusting fluid. The sixty-eight of us bathed at once in this disinfectant. The water was ice-cold. Prison attendants had to pull out the older ones among us who were on the verge of suffocation. There were no SS men around us as we stood there, shivering and waiting for the next step in the procedure—the showers. The prisoners who took care of us were so utterly impersonal that they might have been tending animals rather than fellow-prisoners. They were used to such scenes. They had to be used to them, and when we complained they assured us that the bath was nothing in comparison to other niceties of life in Buchenwald.

Finally the showers were turned on, and water sprayed from ten outlets. Warm water, pleasant, warm, clean water! For ten minutes we scrubbed off the dirt of the disinfectant with some clay-like soap which was provided. Suddenly the water turned cold, freezing cold. We rushed out hurriedly, but the prisoner-attendants forced us back and kept us under the icy flow until we were stiff with cold.

At last it was over. The attendants gave us one towel for each four men. A prisoner in our group who was ill, collapsed when he emerged from the shower. The attendants carried him away and he died that same night.

The Buchenwald system of extermination had already begun operation for us. The attendants told us that an average of eight to ten men had to be hospitalized every day after the showers. It was only a short trip from the hospital to the camp's crematorium, but since everyone was to end up in the crematorium sooner or later, what was the difference?

I began to understand the attitude of some of these veteran prisoners. They had become fatalists as the only means of preserving their sanity. Someday the Nazis would burn them, before death or after; in the meanwhile each did his work, thinking and feeling as little as possible. It was hard to see the future through the walls of Buchenwald. The Nazi program of morale education had succeeded with them; they were without confidence, without belief in human decency. Each owned only one possession—a sick and shabby life.

Next we went to the Kleider Rammer, the Clothing Depot, to receive our convict uniforms. To reach this depot we had to cross a broad courtyard, completely naked, although the temperature was 20 degrees Fahrenheit. The Kleider Kummer resembled a fine clothing store, with polished parquet floors and waxed counters behind which prisoner-employees worked.

We stood in line and one by one the attendants handed us our shirts. At the next counter we each received a pair of pants, any pair, any size, any length, which the attendants flung at us without looking. These were not striped convict clothes. We would have to earn those clothes. We were given clothing turned in by other prisoners, the flimsy rags of hundreds of thousands of anti-Nazis who may have worn them ten years or more before their incarceration. They were civilian clothes, offering a panorama of the styles of the past fifty years, so variously patched that I saw trousers of which one leg was black, one yellow; blue pants with red patches; red pants with a huge white patch on the seat; ancient rabbinical frock coats with one tail missing; jackets with sleeves which fell off when we inserted our arms.

Those who received pants too wide in the waist were particularly unlucky. Since they had neither string nor belts they had to hold the pants up at all times. A tight pair was a much better bargain. In addition to these rags we received worn-out socks and wooden clogs. To complete our attire for the new life they gave us convict numbers with orders to sew them on our jackets and pants. Despite the freezing cold they gave us no overcoats. We were dressed in the official uniform of the quarantine, and a more clownish, rag-tag, bobtail crew would be difficult to imagine.

When we reached the quarantine barracks we found about twelve hundred prisoners. Guards lined us up in five rows. It was time to stand up and be counted, time for the famous Appel. They marched us into the courtyard. The freezing wind whipped across cold stones. It was already dusk. Our teeth chattered uncontrollably, and pangs of hunger accentuated the cold. We regretted not eating every scrap of food when we had the chance.

Appel demanded a strong, well-fed man.

12

A Hungarian acquaintance of mine who was in England at the outbreak of the war once told me how the British conducted the daily roll-call in the camp where he was interned. "They blew a bugle between five and six in the morning to announce the roll-call. They called it the 'count.' We strolled down to the courtyard and lined up in two or three double rows, depending on how many we were. The commandant and his aide came down to conduct the count. They faced us and saluted in a courteous and soldierly manner. Then the commandant would say, 'Good morning, men,' and we answered, in chorus, 'Good morning, sir.' Two sergeants took over and counted us. They made their report to the commandant. He saluted once more, and then said, 'Dismissed!' We returned to the barracks. The whole business usually took five minutes."

This was in England where Oswald Moseley was not in power.

In Buchenwald our first Appel (I don't know why they gave it a French name) was considerably different. I will never be able to forget Appel as long as I live. After twenty minutes of shivering in the cold dim yard I turned to a neighbor and whispered,"

"How much longer will this last?"

"I've only been through two of them so far," he said. He, too, was a new prisoner. "It went on two and a half to three hours each time."

I couldn't believe him at first. It didn't seem possible that we would be kept so long in this bitter weather, dressed in leftover rags. I asked my other neighbor, "Does this really last for hours?"

"Everyone says so. I only got here yesterday."

I looked around. In the faint light I could see that all the men were blue in the face and their eyes watered as the keen wind cut under their lids. I noticed that experience had made the veteran prisoners more resourceful. They did not stand as we did.

They constantly swung from side to side, brushing their freezing bodies against the nearest men to create some slight increase in blood circulation.

Buchenwald was made up of two camps, the Big Lager and the Small Lager. We, in quarantine, were in the Small Lager, while the Big Lager contained those who had been assigned work. The system was to count the Big Lager first, but we had to wait in the courtyard while this was going on. Among us strode the SS troopers in heavy fur-lined coats and fur-lined boots. Yet things were no better in the Big Lager where the men, having worked at inhuman tasks all day, also had to stand in the yard for two or three hours every night. Appel, like the showers, had its daily death toll. The attendants picked up those who collapsed and carted them off (courtyard, hospital, crematorium—the standard itinerary!).

They did not let us alone while we stood there.

The supervisors walked in and out of our ranks, barking orders.

"Keep your heads up!"

"Stand erect!"

"Straighten that line!"

The SS men came by with their flashlights and counted. The younger boys, standing beside their fathers in the line, were crying. Men tried to cover the heads of their sons with the corners of their jackets, or lay their arms over their shoulders. Tears froze on the children's faces and the ice bit deeper into raw chapped skin. There was nothing with which to wipe away the moisture except a coat sleeve.

A Turkish Jew took off his jacket and wrapped it around his fifteen-year-old son while he himself stood there in his torn shirt. The emaciated child was frightened. The prisoner-supervisors ran up to the man and shouted. "Put your coat on! Put it on immediately!" One of them even struck the Turkish father. "If the boy can't stand it, let him freeze!"

I heard another supervisor tell the man, "No sympathy here. Remember that. No sympathy, no mercy. Everyone for himself." Still a third supervisor made a whispered comment to us. He must have felt obliged to explain. "Every day twenty men or more die during the Appel. But if we don't keep this kind of discipline a hundred will die before it's over tonight. Don't forget that."

I chanced one whispered word. "Why?"

"Why? Listen, an incident like this might lengthen the Appel by an hour. An extra hour means a hundred lives."

I began to understand why a father must cease being a father, why we must endure together—yet supremely alone—or freeze to death. After more than two hours of this, as we stood completely numbed, swaying from side to side in a queer a-rhythmical dance, a shouted order brought us up sharply.

"Achtung! Attention!"

The prisoner-supervisors rushed to take their appointed places in line, trying in the meanwhile to force us to keep our rows straight and stand at attention so that the Appel could proceed without a hitch. They shouted at one, struck another to awaken him from the sleep induced by cold. We forced our numb legs into the required position. The block leader hurried to the SS trooper, snapped to attention, and reported, "We are so-

and-so many; such-and-such a number dead." The SS man began to count. At the end of each row, where the supervisors had dragged them, lay the dead. The SS trooper kicked each corpse to make sure there was no shamming. There was none. The dead men were dead.

Then he wrote' a receipt in the block-leader's notebook. In the democracy of Buchenwald he receipted for the dead as well as the living. The block leader saluted once more, received his notebook back, and the SS soldier left.

And so we awaited the end of the ordeal, the dismissal, the return to quarters. But we were not yet finished. There was still the block-leader's speech.

The block-leader, also a prisoner, made his speech once a day for the benefit of newcomers, but we had to listen to it at every evening Appel. He knew it by heart, never changed a word, and to this day I, too, know it by heart, having heard it so many times. He spoke in German and did not consider it important that many newcomers could not understand him. We called it the Installation Speech, and it went, word for word, as follows:

"You have just come here, and don't imagine that you've arrived at some sanitarium. Don't harbor any hopes that you'll soon be leaving. Here at Buchenwald a very difficult life awaits you. Here you must work until your arms break—work hard without stopping. Here you have only one right: the right to work hard and without rest. You must practice comradeship among yourselves because true comradeship is the only thing that will ease things for you a little and make the unrelieved hardship more bearable. When you are given a job, you must make every effort to do it to the satisfaction of your superiors. Don't imagine for one moment that sabotage can be effective. The crematorium is the answer to the most trifling attempt at sabotage. The crematorium is always smoking. That smoke comes from the bodies of your comrades. The same fate awaits anyone here who allows himself the illusion that he can do anything contrary to what he's told. In conclusion, I warn the Jews here that life for them will be even more difficult than for the rest. You have to work harder than the others."

He might have been delivering a funeral oration.

Every word had the dead weight of a sledgehammer. It was as if he had designed his speech as an assault on the slight fortress of our hopes. When the installation speech ended, we had passed three hours in the courtyard.

Then we heard the command, "Dismissed!"

We went into the barracks.

13

After the windy courtyard, paralyzed from the cold, we welcomed the barracks as though it were a mansion. In the middle of the room stood a large iron stove which gave out a delightful warmth. Naturally we all rushed toward it. Nearby stood a long table surrounded by benches. There was one chair next to the stove.

The chair was for the "table chief," another factotum in the grim hierarchy of Buchenwald. Members of our group never got near the stove. The other prisoners who had been in Buchenwald longer made it painfully clear that newcomers were not entitled to the warmth of the fire. The block-leader's talk of comradeship had evidently taken little root among our fellow-prisoners in the barracks. Except for our group of Jews, the others in quarantine were Poles, Ukrainians, Frenchmen, Germans, and other nationalities.

Many of them were what the Nazis wanted them to be: beaten, despairing, tortured, and hopeless. They were men created according to the Nazi blueprint as drawn up by Hitler when he put forward the theory that all non-Germanic nations in Europe must be weakened biologically since there existed no natural German superiority it had to be created by forcing other peoples into a physically and mentally inferior status. We wore patched pants. We wore numbers. We had ludicrously shaven heads. Obviously we were inferior.

In Buchenwald it was a principle to depress the morale of prisoners to the lowest possible level, thereby preventing the development of fellow-feeling or co-operation among the victims. When a prisoner kicked a member of our group away from the stove, he was putting Nazi theory into action.

The entire camp was run with one purpose: to get as much work out of each prisoner on the least possible amount of food. The day's diet, we would soon discover, usually consisted of a small piece of bread, a half-liter of coffee, and a liter of soup. If prisoners died on that diet, it made little difference. There were always more prisoners available.

Our barracks was divided into six sections lying in two wings, Wing A and Wing B. Each wing had a large common dining room furnished with ten bare wooden tables. Since the tables were designed for ten men, quite obviously these thrifty supermen seated twenty to twenty-five at each. It was impossible to eat the wretched food in any semblance of comfort.

We had a common sleeping room with beds arranged in three tiers, bunk fashion. We were about two hundred and thirty men in each wing, and we had between us one hundred and ten beds, each with one blanket. We crowded two, and sometimes three into a bunk, and tried to keep warm under the blanket. The toilet facilities consisted of a common wash-bowl and eight water closet seats to accommodate four hundred and fifty to five hundred men in both wings.

Some men gathered our new group together to show us our bunks and instruct us in the rules of the house. These prisoner-employees bore the title of Room Attendant (Stube Dienst). They indicated the bunk each man was to occupy, and distributed one thin, dirty and ragged blanket to every two men.

The dormitory was unheated and the windows left open to assure fresh air. This system was efficient since those who were not healthy enough to make good prospects for slave labor would soon contract pneumonia, die, and make way for men who could work. We had here, in its pure form, the doctrine of the survival of the fittest applied to man on the animal rather than the civilized level.

That night we received no food whatever since we had only arrived. The first day was always a fast day. "Besides," as some of our fellow-prisoners remarked, "you can't be very hungry. You've only been here one day."

Our room attendant was a decent sort. He showed us our places at the table where we might eat when we eventually received food. He told us "we should sit at the same places to rest ourselves after the Appel. Now we had a place to sleep and a place to eat, and we prepared for night in that chill Thuringian land.

In addition to the numbers which we had sewed on our jackets and pants, we received a small Star of David to attach beside our numbers. The Nazis were evidently determined to preserve the purity of those considered unfit, as well as the purity of the fit, although the crematorium would doubtless eradicate those symbols of our Jewishness in time. Our roommates gazed at us curiously as we sewed on our Stars. Jews had never before been permitted in this barracks so that the inmates had previously gone pure and uncontaminated into the fires. And there were among those beaten men, sitting on death's doorstep, more than one who became distinctly cool toward us when they discovered we were Jewish.

Here it was again! Comradeship in prison started as a continuation of the sort of comradeship one had led in his previous life. We who had fought side by side in the Resistance, who had faced the common enemy shoulder to shoulder, understood that every cleavage among us carried grist to the Nazi mill.

The same was true of all previously organized or politically active people in that barracks, but the great "individualists" of our free days, the unorganized and backward workers, the cynics, not to mention business men who knew nothing of organized action (they were among us, too), all disintegrated morally. They became witless tools for the Nazis. They groveled for favors although their groveling degraded them still further. And they did not live long in Buchenwald!

There were really few Jews in Buchenwald since none had been brought there since 1941. Before that it had been a murder camp for thousands of German and Austrian Jews, all except three hundred and fifty of whom had died in Buchenwald or were sent to the Auschwitz gas chambers. The three hundred and fifty turned out to be skilled and useful workers whom the Nazis needed, mostly stone masons who built the Buchenwald munitions plant, officers' apartments, and other important buildings. Although they slept in segregated barracks they worked together with Gentile prisoners, sharing the democracy of labor.

When our companions in the barracks discovered that we were all political prisoners, some of them immediately became more friendly and confidential. This was especially true of the Russian and Czech prisoners. The Ukrainians, however, all "White Russian" emigres who had lived abroad before the war, looked down on us and behaved very disagreeably. They would share nothing with us except the brutality of the treatment they received in Buchenwald. They thought they could survive alone, never seeing their own flesh in the smoke that always rose lazily from the crematorium.

14

My number was 22383.

Prisoner 22383 soon became familiar with the fantastic geography of Buchenwald. Like every man with a number I soon came to know the many courtyards in the camp. In one of these stood a solidly built and well-furnished stone house, the home of the Elite Guard (SS) officer who was in charge of the crematorium. The location was convenient. It was close to the officer's place of work and if he so chose, he could look out of his curtained windows and assure himself that the crematorium was still functioning.

The officer didn't live alone in his fine house. He shared its delights with his wife and children, and they too could look out after dinner to watch the smoke from the crematorium's chimney make a pattern against the sunset. His children grew up in that house; there he ate and drank, slept with his wife, listened to his phonograph.

Other SS officers lived in a neighboring courtyard, well within sight and sound of the crematorium. These officers' homes were a small part of a camp which covered forty square kilometers and provided facilities for more than twenty thousand men.

The fundamental plan of the camp was its division into the Small Lager and the Big Lager. We could not go from the Small Lager to the Big Lager without a special permit since the Small Lager contained quarantined prisoners and other temporary inmates who were kept there only a few days before departing to various work camps in other parts of Germany.

Officially the Big Lager was a "political camp," but actually a little less than half of the inmates were political prisoners—confirmed anti-Nazis, Resistance fighters, labor leaders, Socialists, Communists, democrats. This explained in part the attitude of many of the prisoners. The "non-politicals" had been brought to Buchenwald from German penal institutions. In the main they were black marketers, profiteers who did not give the Nazis a big enough cut, and deserters from the

Army. Among them were also "Bible Readers," members of a religious sect who would not bear arms or work in war industry. Their fathers had refused service in the Kaiser's Army and they did not care to make an exception of Hitler. They were comparable to the Nazarenes in Hungary.

The Nazis executed many "Bible Readers," but the group held to their beliefs without wavering, and finally, in the summer of 1943, they were assigned work their religion allowed them to perform. The non-political prisoners included Verbrechery convicts who were serving life sentences for robbery or murder. Being Germans they lived in separate barracks, but on Sundays and holidays they mingled with the other captives hi the yard.

Every prisoner wore a colored triangle on his coat to indicate the category in which he belonged. The political prisoners wore a red triangle, the criminals green, and the murderers gray with the letter K super-imposed. Nazi science also decreed Buchenwald as a cure for homosexuality, and homosexuals, all Germans or Austrians, wore blue triangles. The Jews wore the

Star of David together with the other insignia. Above the triangle was each prisoner's number. When we met in the courtyard our emblems did away with the necessity for a great deal of preliminary conversation.

There were two Russian groups in the camp. One group comprised Russian civilians, mainly emigres, nationalist Ukrainian kulaks and landowners, Czarist leftovers who had been stranded in Germany, and a few who had tried to play the quisling.

They hated the Soviets, and as a result the Nazis rewarded them with the type of work usually reserved for hangmen. Many had joined the Vlassov Russian Nazi SS group. The traitor Vlassov had once been a Soviet officer of Ukrainian origin, and he led his SS men against his homeland. The irony was that many of these Ukrainians, completely unable to maintain discipline in their SS Division, ended up in Buchenwald as a reward for their services to Hitler. There was no group in the camp of whom we were more contemptuous.

The other Russian group consisted of prisoners-of-war. They wore no numbers or letters. Their uniform was their designation and they wore it proudly.

For the most part they were young men, clean-cut and orderly. Even the Nazis respected them. They had their own barracks. They worked, but their officers did their jobs in separate buildings or in the administrative offices. The skilled workers among the Russians worked in the various shops, the hospital, or in supervisory positions in the offices. This group had a hatred of the Ukrainians that matched their hatred of the Nazis, and on more than one occasion they took action against the Vlassovites.

There were fifty-nine barracks in the Big Lager, all of wood, all identical inside and out, down to the last item of furniture. Each barracks had a capacity of three hundred men—and housed anywhere from four hundred to four hundred and eighty.

The five stone buildings in the area included a huge modernized kitchen building (Heftlings Kueche), a laundry of similar proportions, the Workers' Statistical Office (Arbeiter Statistik), the political and police administration offices, and the enormous food and clothing stores.

There were also some tremendous stone barracks which quartered about four thousand soldiers, but these buildings could not be considered part of the prison proper. The soldiers had their own kitchens, officers' apartments, and library. Among their stone barracks was the beautiful villa in which the commandant of Buchenwald lived with his wife. The villa was so luxurious that it looked as though it had been lifted from some spacious lawn and dropped in the middle of Buchenwald.

The eight hundred guards had a separate barracks. There was an arms depot on the prison grounds, and a hospital with four hundred beds (and twelve hundred patients). We prisoners even had a movie-house with a seating capacity of five hundred where we could see Nazi films, and a library containing twenty-five thousand volumes of disgusting paeans to Nazi degeneracy.

And we prisoners at Buchenwald were not completely unloved! We were also provided with a prisoners' brothel employing thirty women!

Of all the buildings in Buchenwald, one was easily the most beautiful and impressive of all. It was of stone, and its handsome windows gave it the appearance of a crystal palace. The walls were inlaid with mosaic, soft rugs covered the floors, and masterpieces of modern craftsmanship filled its rooms.

This magnificent edifice was the Experimental Station: Block 51. Here the Nazi scientists performed experiments, not on rats or rabbits, but on healthy people since there were more of these at hand and they were easier to catch. Whoever went to Block 51 played the guinea pig for a few weeks, before departing for the crematorium. Nazi scientists removed hearts from the bodies of men to see how long these organs would function outside the body. They took out a prisoner's lungs and tested artificial lungs in their place. They injected the helpless prisoners with a variety of experimental serums. They removed the genitals or the liver from living humans to test the reaction. After the liberation, the Allies found thousands of jars of formaldehyde containing organs extracted from living prisoners.

German efficiency was no less evident in Block 51 than elsewhere. Every formaldehyde jar carried a label bearing the victim's name, age, and "race."

Peter Unschlag, Aryan, 35 years old. Moritz Schwartz, Jew, 55 years old. And on one jar, in which was preserved the heart of a Jew, was a notation that the victim's wife had been an "Aryan." The Nazis did not explain what effect this had on the bottled heart.

The crematorium, one of the better buildings, had a twelve-meter chimney which never stopped smoking. Thirty-five men worked there. Their duties consisted of burning corpses or dissecting them when so ordered by physicians, and extracting morsels of gold or platinum from the teeth of the dead. During this phase of their operations guards kept the workers under constant supervision to prevent them from appropriating a stray gold filling.

This explained why clerks in Buchenwald recorded exactly how much gold or platinum we had in our mouths, the precise location of every bridge, every filling. The Nazis prepared themselves for the possession of this dental gold well in advance, confident that it would be theirs sooner or later.

Mass executions took place in a large room designed for that purpose in the crematorium. The method of execution was amazingly like that used to dispose of cattle in the Chicago stockyards. Prisoners did not walk into this room. They were thrust down a dark chute which opened on the chamber, and as each victim reached the bottom of this grisly kelly-slide, a crematorium employee struck him violently over the head with a blunt instrument. In a brief time the room would be filled with dead, half dead, or insensate people who were then placed on a moving belt which brought their bodies into the cremating hall where attendants stripped them of their clothes and their dental gold. If the person had neither gold nor platinum in his mouth he was immediately thrust, still warm, into one of the ovens.

Eight furnaces, each with two ovens, were constantly blazing. The rules of the crematorium allowed twelve minutes for each body to be reduced to ashes.

Other centers of endeavor in the camp included the carpentry shop where thirteen hundred men worked, and a locksmith shop where six to eight hundred skilled men labored day and night on twelve-hour shifts.

A factory on the grounds turned out rockets—the famous V-l and V-2 buzz bombs. The factory was located in the section of the camp that included the officers' apartment houses, pleasant stone structures surrounded by gardens, which gave the immediate area all the appearance of a pleasant small town.

This section lay outside the main gate in a space about eight kilometers in width. It was impossible to leave the prison without passing through this area, even if a prisoner managed to run the gauntlet of the charged wire. Escape was almost impossible. In all the time I passed in Buchenwald only three men escaped, two of whom were soon caught. We never heard of the third again. The charged wire seldom served its purpose since the guards shot anyone who approached it.

Among the list of forbidden activities in Buchenwald was suicide. Only the Nazis had the right to a prisoner's life or his gold teeth.

The last structure in the camp was the freight train station where supplies came in and goods produced in the camp were shipped out. Prisoners who worked outside the camp traveled to work on these trains. SS troopers and police dogs guarded them.

The dogs had been trained to jump for the throat and bite through the windpipe. More than once a Nazi guard who got out of the wrong side of his bed, or didn't like the shape of a prisoner's ears, signaled his dog to perform his trick. And when a guard received a new dog he naturally wanted to test the animal's efficiency. On whom could he test it if not a prisoner? The officials never called anyone to account for these sportive killings.

When the dogs finished their midday meal of one kilo of beef each, the prisoners often fought among themselves savagely, struggling for a bone on which to gnaw.

This was Buchenwald, its atmosphere, its environs.

15

After we returned to the quarantine barracks following the first night's Appel, twenty-four of us, including myself, were chosen to go to the kitchen in the morning to fetch coffee for the men. At ten o'clock that night, cold and exhausted, yet hungry, we crawled into our narrow bunks and went to sleep.

The regular rising hour was four a.m., but guards awoke the kitchen detail at three-thirty. Stripped to the waist, we washed at the common washbowl and dried ourselves as best we could with the one towel allotted every four men. We had no soap since soap —or what the Nazis called soap—was only for men who worked. The attendant hurried us. We put on our rags and then set out for the kitchen, walking in rows of five. We groped our way through the dark, following the attendant who carried a small flashlight.

When we reached the kitchen entrance we found a large crowd already waiting. Every barracks sent twenty-four men to the kitchen, and there were one hundred .and thirty-five barracks in this part of the camp. The groups entered the kitchen according to barracks number. Our number was 53. We waited a half hour in the bitter cold before it was our turn.

After that wait the kitchen was delightfully warm and even the odor of the ersatz coffee, from steaming forty-liter cans, was appetizing. The kitchen was brilliantly lit but all the windows were carefully blacked out.

We took our twelve containers of coffee, two men to each, formed four rows at the kitchen door, and started back in military formation. After frequent pauses to rest we arrived at the barracks, our eyes watering from the cold of the winter dawn, our hands scalded by spilt coffee since we had stumbled many times on the unfamiliar path.

It was half past four when we arrived back and our roommates, fully dressed, were waiting for us. Each man received a half-liter of coffee. Those who went to work also received a small piece of bread. The rest of us would have to wait until eight o'clock for the bread ration.

Then—the morning Appel!

We had just survived the prolonged torture of one Appel, managed to squeeze in a few hours of sleep, and here it was again!

It was a repetition of the previous night's Appel with little change in the technique or even the incidents. We stood in the yard, the icy dawn numbing our bodies, for three hours. Our wooden clogs gave our feet no warmth and our tattered hand-me-downs seemed even less protection than they had the night before. The inmates of the Big Lager went through the ordeal first; then the working prisoners; and finally the men in quarantine who still had a little of the outside world's vitality left in their bodies.

Those winter Appels were actually a form of extermination. Certainly they represented a standard means of killing off prisoners and making way for new ones. In addition to those who regularly fell dead during Appel, there were every day a number who contracted pneumonia and subsequently died. Buchenwald did not delay its work. In the first twenty-four hours three of our group of sixty-eight collapsed during Appel.

When our first morning Appel ended at eight o'clock we couldn't go inside because men were cleaning the barracks. We found what little relief we could by walking rapidly back and forth, swinging our arms, jumping up and down. We looked in each other's faces and I think we were all shocked to see the changes wrought by one day in Buchenwald. Even the young boys had aged physically. My friend Nicholas Sapir, who usually had an indomitable sense of humor, now walked about with a long face and an air of hopelessness, staring with empty eyes at friends or strangers. Some of our Turkish friends wept and pretended that the cold wind brought tears to their eyes. Precz, who had once escaped from an earlier transport, muttered quietly, partly to us, partly to himself, "Damn it, you should have let me escape. We can't stand this long. If three of us go every day, how many Appels will it take to kill us all off?"

Doubtless it was in some such form that the Nazis presented mathematical problems to their school children. "All right, Hans, if three men die in one Appel, and there are two Appels every day, how many days will it take to kill sixty-eight men?"

At nine o'clock we were finally permitted to return to the barracks where the room attendants distributed knives, a small bread ration, and a pat of margarine. Each of us sliced his bread carefully, saving a piece to make another meal, but no matter how we tried to stretch that crust or keep our hunger in check not a scrap was left in an hour's time. Tomorrow we would show more forbearance, or so we thought. At four in the afternoon we would get a little soup.

After breakfast—that was the name for it—we went to the political police office where we underwent a detailed interrogation during which we described every detail of our lives from our birth to our arrest. Photographers took our pictures, full-face and profile, with convict numbers across our chests and a two day growth of beard to add to our sinister appearance. These were not photographs of which a man would order enlargements.

We did not mind this examination because the room was warm and comfortable. We could speak our own language, too, since the prisoner-interrogators were of every nationality. Their thoroughness was typical of everything in Buchenwald, but the heat was so welcome that we lingered over macabre details concerning our gold and platinum dental fillings.

It was half past four before we received our ration of soup. Steckruhbe Suppe they call it, and I think it was made of beets. At any rate it was hot and therefore we enjoyed it.

Following this meal, officials informed us that we would no longer mix with the "Aryans" in quarantine. The next day we would go to the Jewish Block where we would be promoted at once to the rank of full-fledged prisoners, and assigned work. Those who could work would receive overcoats.

In the morning we got our little piece of bread. Then we stood in line and marched off to Block 22, the ghetto within a ghetto.

16

Wherever there is a survivor of Buchenwald, the name of Emil Korlbach survives. Emil was the young Block Leader of the Jewish Block.

When we first arrived at the Jewish Block the working day had already begun and we found only the attendants and a few sick prisoners. The clerk entered our names on the lists. The attendants divided the sixty-five men into two groups and assigned us accommodations in the two wings of the Block, A Fluegel and B Fluegel. Here we were accorded certain delicate privileges: a father and son might share a bed, or brother and brother, or friend and friend.

The attendants were all German Jews. A man named Kurt received us. He was substituting for Emil Korlbach. Emil was sick at the time, and in the hospital, but we were in the Block only a few minutes before we felt his influence.

Our welcome there was little different from the other Buchenwald welcomes we had experienced.

We met the same coolness, the same indifference and even unfriendliness. Meeting this sullen inhospitality from Jews confused and disheartened us. Had we invaded Buchenwald of our own will, intruded upon the idyllic peace of these men, disturbed their comfort in any way, we might have understood their attitude. But what had we done to be received like intruders? It was not enough that the Nazis were hounding us to death, tormenting us in concentration camps, while quisling Ukrainians and German "Aryans" looked at us with hatred! One would think it was our little group, and not Chamberlain, who had conferred with Hitler in Berchtesgaden. How else explain that here in the Jewish Block everyone spoke to us over his shoulder?

At last we came upon a seventy-four-year-old Hungarian prisoner who was willing to talk to us. He was convalescing from an injury sustained at work. The old man had lived forty years in Germany, working as a Berlin cabinet maker. His two sons-in-law were Gentiles now serving in the German Army. Two months previously the Nazis had detained him and his wife, ostensibly to deport them to Hungary. Instead they had been "concentrated" in a camp near Berlin. Then they had sent him to Buchenwald, and his wife to the women's camp at Ravensbruck (the destination, as we later learned, of the women we had left behind in Malin).

The old man told us that a group similar to ours, comprising sixty Hungarian, Rumanian, and Turkish Jews, had arrived ten days before us. Of that group, nineteen were now dead. The Jews in this Block, Block 22, had lived "peacefully" for the past two years during which time no new prisoners had arrived. We were the first few newcomers. We were crowding the quarters. Changes like this upset the men in Buchenwald, unbalanced them, and raised again the fear of the unknown, impending changes, deportations, Auschwitz, the crematorium.

In Buchenwald the status quo meant life.

The old Hungarian had fallen into a pit on his very first day of work on a construction job. His leg had swollen severely, and other prisoners brought him back to the Block. "I got three days Schonung (indulgence)," he said, "so I can rest here that long.

But I don't get much pleasure out of it. The men are rough with me. The attendants push you around and kick you on the least pretense. They have no patience for old people like me. They're always saying, 'You've lived long enough anyway, old man."

The Block Leader is very strict. He scares us all to death. They took him to the hospital for some kind of a small operation but I suppose he'll be back soon."

As he spoke we could detect undertones in his voice. Clearly he wished the Block Leader might never return from the hospital to plague him.

This was the first reference to Emil Korlbach that I heard, the same Emil who immediately in 1933, at the age of nineteen, was clapped into prison by Hitler's Gestapo. From that day on he had lived in the shadow of the gallows, the blank wall of the firing squad, the charged wire of Buchenwald. Ten years—his entire early manhood. And now, by the old man's testimony, he was some sort of fierce and relentless man, hardened by suffering, steeled by experience.

I soon found that everyone called him simply Emil. Some loved him. Some hated him. Everyone felt his presence throughout the entire camp, including the SS officers, the crematorium attendants, and the children of the commandant.

In the course of its existence twenty-three thousand men left Buchenwald alive, and no one can count how many of these thousands owe their fives to Emil Korlbach. He was a veteran prisoner. He had learned how to be a prisoner under the Nazis and this was a science in itself. He knew their principles, their rules. He understood what passed for their souls. He divined their maddest motivations. He walked among them with his head high and with never a sign of fear, yet the Nazis had double reason to hate him. Emil was a Communist, and Emil was a Jew.

Yet they did not kill him. On the contrary, they accepted his authority. It was not till many months had passed that I discovered all this, and still later I found out that the majority of the prisoners never did know of all the feats he accomplished. That was part of his technique of knowing how to be a prisoner in Buchenwald.

Personal experience taught everyone that Emil was severe, hard, a disciplinarian. When Emil gave an order it had to be carried out, there were no two ways about it. And he gave orders which were at times merciless and unbearable to men already over-driven. It seemed incomprehensible.

Emil was following a policy. What was the purpose of Buchenwald? Death. What was the answer to Buchenwald? Life. Emil's goal was simple: to save as many lives as possible. That, and no more. Emil knew how to do the job! He knew that only the utmost severity with men, and even the whip, would keep them alive. We were not on the earth, among human beings. The rules of the outside world were useless.

Imagine that you are Emil Korlbach. You are a prisoner in Buchenwald. In your charge are four hundred men. They are bitter, desperate, unbalanced. They have no reason to hope for anything good in life. They drag the heavy burden of their existence from one day to the next. Behind them, like as not, are memories of friends and family, all whom they loved, now dead. Before them lies the prospect of that dreadful' twelve-minute tenancy of the crematorium ovens. But you are Emil. You are responsible for these four hundred. You have to keep them alive. That means you have to maintain order or the Nazis will kill them. They are starving. Many are dying of hunger. You have to force half dead men to work because if you do not—the crematorium. And it is not only their physical life you must keep alive. It is their spiritual life, their mental life, as well. You have to believe that there is a future for these men in which they can play a positive role. There is little left in them to love, and yet you must love them.

There are very few men who could have been an Emil Korlbach.

I remember evenings when Emil would talk to men in the Jewish Block, explaining some apparently heartless command he had given them. "I know some of you detest me," he said. "You think I'm playing up to the Nazis at your expense. I don't care what you think. But just remember this: do as I tell you if you want to stay alive, or even if you don't. I want you to stay alive and I'll see to it that you do."

His leadership in this Block was not the only thing that distinguished him. Emil also accomplished other impossibilities. It was he who helped make Buchenwald the one concentration camp in which there was an active, functioning Underground.

Naturally many men understood Emil and therefore loved him. This was true not only in our Block but in every Block where prisoners in leadership knew him, for he was one of the key members of the small band who directed the Underground activities in Buchenwald.

The Underground had the aim which Emil expressed: its one function was to save lives, and they often accomplished this by misleading or tricking the SS and the guards. This was also the genesis of most of Emil's harsh orders. It was as impermissible to disobey a Block Leader as an SS trooper.

I heard many conflicting opinions about Emil while he was in the hospital. Some had a natural reaction which I could appreciate: they instinctively distrusted the prisoner-representatives whom the Nazis themselves appointed, and they knew from bitter experience that some of these men, in fear only of their own lives, were on occasion as ruthless as the SS guards. The German tactic was to place criminal elements in positions of power: murderers, arsonists, rapists, convicts of every stripe. They hoped thereby to encourage the prisoners to do the work of killing each other off, and in many cases this policy was successful, particularly in the early days of Buchenwald.

When Emil arrived in 1937, the Block Leaders were just such criminal elements, while the majority of the prisoners were leaders of anti-Nazi organizations. The first task the political prisoners undertook was to wrest leadership from the criminals. They succeeded to a large extent, partly because the Nazis needed internal discipline as much as they needed mutual murder.

When I arrived at Buchenwald—and this is knowledge I did not have at the time—Emil and about twenty other Block Leaders worked together, keeping each other informed of the Nazis' plans.

The Underground had to counteract these plans. It was the crudest task that any Underground has ever faced because the method was to devise a way to sacrifice one or two men to save fifty—or fifty men to save five hundred. The Nazi system was so thorough that anti-Nazis, too had to use death as a tool.

Even in Buchenwald some currents of civilian life persisted. The Underground was separated into two factions! One was composed of Communists, sympathizers, and other left-wingers, all veteran, experienced prisoners. The other group had no Communist members and was even ideologically anti-Communist. Yet in the proximity of an SS uniform there was little time for ideological discussion. Both organizations shared the same aim, and neither tried to undermine the other. There was a working agreement between the two which brought results.

17

At three in the afternoon of our first day the attendants picked some of us to help distribute the evening meal. It was customary for them to call upon the sick or upon new arrivals to help them with this chore. Twenty of us marched off to the kitchen, this time in broad daylight. We were happy to help. It occupied our minds, and besides we were ravenously hungry.

We went through the same routine we followed when we had gone for the breakfast coffee, waiting outside the kitchen for our barracks number to be called. Again the food, which I knew to have been foul, smelled positively enticing in the warm building. Kitchen helpers distributed supper in tubs which weighed about forty-five kilograms each. We lugged these tubs back to the barracks.

Then the attendants gave us each an enameled dish for soup, a pint sized can for coffee, and a spoon and knife for each pair of men. Then and there they marked the utensils with the name and number of the prisoner to whom they belonged. Any exchange of dishes was against regulations.

Each of us had a small locker in the barracks, and now the attendants handed each of us a bolt. But the bolt was unnecessary. We always left the lockers open. I noticed that many lockers contained some bread, or perhaps an onion or other odd bits of food such as a half strip of bacon. These belonged to prisoners of long standing who were permitted to receive an occasional package from the outside. We stared enviously at these delicacies, longing for the day when we, too, could receive packages.

The locker doors were open. The treasures were within easy reach. My group and I could approach them at will but we could never, under any circumstances, help ourselves.

Rules of the Lager, self-imposed rules, were stern, horrible—and necessary. If hunger so demoralized a man that he stole another's bread, no one reported him to the SS or even to the Block

Leader. The room attendants themselves took care of him so thoroughly that never again would he be capable of pilfering. If he did not die of the beating, they so incapacitated him that he was fit only for the crematorium, or Auschwitz. That is why the men never used the bolts.

Emil and his companions approved of this rule because it actually helped us maintain a certain standard of morale and mutual trust. After all, we had been sentenced to starvation. A man who stole helped execute the Nazi sentence against us. Without such rules the Blocks in the Big Lager would have sunk to the same level as those in the Small Lager where such self-discipline did not exist, and dirt and typhus killed hundreds every day.

At half past five that day we caught a glimpse of our own future when the working prisoners returned to the Block. Many of them were middle-aged and elderly men. They were thoroughly exhausted. They talked little. They wolfed the miserable scraps of food, left-over bread, and then dragged themselves to the washbowls to clean up a little. Washing, too, under any circumstances, was a factor in morale.

No sooner did they finish than the whistle blew.

It was now six-twenty. Evening Appel!

We lined up in the courtyard.

Suddenly we heard music, the music of Buchenwald! A brass band!

Of all the camp's grim facilities, the band was perhaps the grimmest. The band members, dressed in Hussar uniforms, were picked musicians led by a famous Czech conductor. They played well, but for them to play at all was a horror in itself. We knew that listening to the blaring horns as we stood at Appel were at least twenty men who would be lying dead, at the end of the ranks, when the count ended.

There was something supremely horrible in dinning into their ears this last blatant note of Kultur as they stood there, dying on their feet. The band mocked every breath we took.

The musicians were always with us. When we marched out to morning Appel thereafter, the band played rollicking tunes. When the men set out for work the musicians piped them on their way; when they returned at evening the band stood at the left of the courtyard and gaily marched us indoors; and at night their cold music announced the end of another day's misery.

The members of the orchestra did no other work. They rehearsed all day, between performances, and from time to time they gave concerts for the "entertainment" of the inmates.

"You see," the SS men would say, "they complain, and yet we Germans give them music!"

Yes, the Germans even provided music at Auschwitz. We met musicians who had played in Auschwitz concerts. There the Nazis would assemble groups of two hundred people, tiny children, women, old men, the incapacitated, give them towels and soap, and tell them they were taking them to the showers. Then SS guards would cram them like sardines into the gas chambers. The doors would close and the victims, facing sudden unexpected death, would cry out, wail, and screech insanely.

But the noise might disturb those on the outside, or ruffle the fine spirits of the commandant. At such moments the band would play loud piercing music. They played for six minutes, no more, no less, because six minutes was quite enough. Then the musicians could rest.

At Appel our Buchenwald band stood one hundred paces from the crematorium as they played.

"See, we even give them music!"

This day Appel took only two hours. An unseen officer occupied most of the time by calling twenty-five prisoners by number through the loudspeaker, and ordering them to report at the door of the barracks.

"Sofort zum Thuere!"

Men so chosen by the impersonal loudspeaker were those who had committed some misdemeanor in the course of the day. These men often returned, but more often they didn't. Prisoners who did not obey the loudspeaker at once, or who crept slowly, sick and exhausted, toward the place of danger, earned a repeated burst from the loudspeaker.

"Der Haefling Nummer 109876 sofort zum Thuere, aber lebhaft!"

Step lively, lively! You might miss something!

Many prisoners did not understand German, and so the business proceeded slowly despite the threats.

Until these men responded the count could not begin. Meanwhile the supervisors rushed busily among us.

"Straighten those lines!"

"Stop moving!"

"Heads in line!"

An hour and a half of this, and then the order: "Achtung! Blok 22 Achtung!"

Kurt, Emil's substitute, stepped forward to report, giving us one last order before presenting himself to the SS trooper: "Muetzen ab!"

"Off with your caps!"

Whenever an SS man appeared we were obliged to bare our heads regardless of the weather. If the Nazis could not win respect, they could order it. The report, the count, the entry in the notebook, on with the caps again, at ease, forward march, back to the Block.

The band played a quick march.

18

The tragedy of the Jewish intellectuals in our Block was the tragedy of all people who live under the illusion that isolation is individualism. Again we had before us the spectacle of the "individualist" who was the very first to lose his individuality and sink into the deepest and most mortal of moods in Buchenwald.

Of the two hundred and sixty prisoners of long standing in the Jewish Block, many were Hungarian, German, and Czech intellectuals. They all worked as stone-masons at the camp's various building projects, a trade they had learned inside the walls of Buchenwald. Among them were doctors, lawyers, architects, painters, a famous Prague Professor of Medicine, and a well-known German screen writer. Their heads were shaved clean except for the strip in the middle, their garments shabby, their faces haggard, starved, almost deformed. Once they had counted for something in the world of culture but they were now amorphous prisoners, irascible, moody, each living only for himself.

Since they never had a perspective of social struggle they had naturally lost interest in everything. They bore their yoke hopelessly, without any faith in the future. Intolerable suffering, mental and physical torture, had sapped their energies.

When we spoke to them they were irritated and they replied rudely. Yet something brought these men to life during our first day there. I still remember the scene clearly as it took place shortly before the whistle for Appel sounded. Each man had cleaned his dishes. Small groups had formed around the tables, cliques of two years' standing. The conversation was desultory. The men sat motionless.

Like couples who have been married for fifty years, they had nothing more to say, having long since discovered all there was to know of each other.

Then the six children who arrived with our group, all of them boys of fourteen to sixteen, seated themselves around the table. They were looking for a little food and they sniffed like hungry puppies. One of the men noticed the boys and pointed them out to the others at the tables. These were the first children in the Jewish Block since the original two hundred and sixty prisoners had arrived!

The men lifted their heads to look. And then the sun somehow broke in the gray and bitter darkness of Buchenwald. Here and there a wrinkled face smiled, a tiny flame flickered in eyes that were lifeless. Each man saw his own children in these six boys, and memories of the outside world finally broke through the prison of their despair. Almost every prisoner had been a family man, and with the exception of the few whose wives were Gentile, they had lost their entire families.

One by one the old-timers arose, still without speaking. They went to their lockers and brought out the little food they had saved—pieces of bacon, salami, biscuits, onions—and pressed the food into the boys' hands. Others brought the youngsters some warm underclothing which they had received from the outside, and some even gave their thin jackets to the children to help them withstand Appel.

Then I realized that the men were not yet dead.

The presence of the children did what none of us could do by ourselves. It created a friendlier relationship between the older prisoners and ourselves.

We did our best to adapt ourselves to the others who accepted the children as common property, a common responsibility. The youngsters, too, desperately needed the security they found in the feeling that they each had two hundred fathers in Buchenwald.

Before we went to bed that night we asked Kurt, Emil's substitute, when we, the newcomers, might go to work. He told us that it wouldn't be before Emil's return from the hospital. Furthermore there was a new regulation which required us to receive a series of injections before we could work.

Kurt also commented on what he thought were some significant improvements in Buchenwald.

Previously mass executions had been a daily occurrence, but news of the brutalities practised in camp had leaked out, and the Swiss Red Cross protested. As an appeasing gesture, the commandant was removed. His removal brought to light his large-scale embezzlement, carried on at the expense of funds provided for prisoners' food and supplies. He had, for example, appropriated thousands of Red Cross packages intended for the prisoners, and sold them for his own profit outside the camp.

The new commandant was a high ranking SS officer named Herman Pister. Pister had instituted better conditions, "better," of course, being a strictly comparative term. There were no more daily mass executions. Guards no longer had official permission to beat prisoners on the job, and whatever beatings we would receive would be purely unofficial.

I believe that other factors, in addition to the Red Cross complaint, inspired this sudden attack of conscience. The Nazis were not unaware that the Russians were then in Poland and moving ahead with inexorable singleness of purpose. This might even have explained a new regulation which Kurt welcomed as one of the great advances in our welfare: skilled Jewish workers would be allowed to work in the factories and shops. This was something to anticipate, no matter how long it might take. Our hopes rose. Surely the Germans must be in desperate need of trained workers if they permitted Jews to work for them. And if their need were so dire, then we could begin to hope for victory and liberation.

While we were kept idle in the barracks we made ourselves useful by helping the room attendants with the cleaning. In return they gave us a little food and even a few cigarettes, the most precious of luxuries. Usually six of us shared one cigarette made of newspaper and some stinking tobacco. We smoked in the toilet, the only place where it was permitted.

But now we each had one long real cigarette to smoke. We clinched the butts to take our pleasure in stages.

After the fourth morning's Appel the loudspeaker announced that new arrivals must go to receive their injections. Kurt quickly lined us up and we set out double-time for the hospital. There were about five hundred men in the line. Two prisoner-doctors and two prisoner-nurses appeared, and unpacked syringes. They ordered us to undress.

This order disturbed us. The preparations were sinister and we had heard many authenticated stories of prisoners killed with the needle, but we calmed down when we saw the men dress and walk briskly away after receiving their shots.

The doctors injected a long needle, first in the right and then the left breast. One long indrawn breath and it was over. In two hours all five hundred of us had received injections. We were to receive four more double injections in the next ten days.

We were to be protected against every conceivable illness since an epidemic at the camp would affect SS men equally with prisoners.

They had no injection, however, to protect us from the beatings, the hunger, and the Appel. To the last day we died without the aid of illness.

19

Emil Korlbach was waiting for us in the Block when we returned from the hospital.

Tall, ascetic, strong-featured, this man immediately gave the impression of one who had lived through suffering. Like all Block Leaders he wore a semi-military uniform—blue soldier's jacket, breeches, and boots. His bearing, too, was that of a soldier. He had great physical self-control. On his face was the story of the years of his youth, spent in imprisonment. Already twenty-nine, Emil had never been able to test the carefree adventures of the young, to savor a first love, perhaps to marry. Emil never had the time to be young.

His father had been a rabbi in Frankfurt-am-Main. When Emil was sixteen he joined the young workers' movement in Germany, and shortly acquired a reputation as a Marxist lecturer. In 1933 he was as well-known to the Nazis as to

Marxist workers, and the Gestapo picked him up soon after Hitler seized power.

The prison number which appeared on his jacket was proof of this. The number was 430. The difference between that 430 and my 22743 explained a great deal. His parents, his brothers and sisters, his relatives, and millions of his people were all dead. And yet he stood confidently before us, erect, a statue poured of steel, and spoke a few words.

"Listen to me." He talked simply, not choosing his words, but as though he were having a casual conversation with old friends. "You're not going to work yet. But I want you to be clear about one thing. When you go to work you've got to hold your own. You can't give them any excuse to say that a Jew can't work as well as an 'Aryan.' It's very important for you to show that we Jews can do what others can do. Right now this is particularly important.

There's a possibility that they're going to open the factories and shops to us before long. That can make life in Buchenwald a lot more bearable for all of us. We can't miss the chance.

"One other thing. I want you to be very careful about keeping clean. I know it's hard but it's got to be done. Keep an eye on each other in this respect. If a disease gets a foothold in this crowded barracks, we're finished. Absolutely finished. Don't forget the crematorium."

When he finished speaking he turned on his heel and headed for Wing B where he had a small room of his own from which he directed the activities of the four hundred men in his care, working from four in the morning until midnight. We were all a little surprised at his manner, so military, so cool, his bearing so measured. He seemed positively Prussian.

We talked about Emil, talked without knowing the many things we have since learned. Only Emil's most trusted friends and companions knew that he was one of the leading members of the Buchenwald Underground. Fully eighty per cent of the camp had not even the slightest suspicion of this. While most of the prisoners surrendered all hope during the first few weeks of their captivity, Emil and his colleagues, men with experience in organization and anti-fascist struggle, were convinced that we would finally annihilate the Nazis. But they knew we would never annihilate them with apathy.

The Underground, like everything else in Buchenwald, was totally different from the Underground in the outside world. What I would have considered an act of great heroism in the Belgian Resistance would be an act of the grossest stupidity, if not an outright provocation, in Buchenwald. We could not use the weapons available in the outside world. In the Resistance we had organized sabotage. In Buchenwald we would not even tolerate talk of sabotage, and if we were convinced a man was intent upon committing an act of sabotage, we would get him out of the way ourselves. One fool, throwing a handful of sand in the oil, would send fifty men to the crematorium.

In the early days Emil and his associates actually worked harder than other prisoners in order to win leading positions and even gain the confidence of the SS. At first many experienced workers, from the trade union movement and the left political parties, could not see what path to follow. There were theories that the function of the Underground should be to sabotage Buchenwald war industry, and there were early misunderstandings and complications which took valuable time before the Underground straightened them out. These misconceptions and delays cost many lives.

Once the Underground agreed on its basic "save-lives" policy, Emil and his associates worked in various ways. Members of the Underground held a number of key administrative positions. They were trustworthy and devoted anti-fascists, Germans in the main, veteran political prisoners. At times they changed a dead man's record and number for the record and number of someone who was living but sentenced to die. This saved one person from the crematorium. Sometimes they found it possible to use bribery, and on occasion even a form of blackmail was effective with certain individuals in authority who had something to conceal.

In addition to Emil, there were two other outstanding leaders of the Underground. One was Sivert, a German Communist, who had also been a prisoner since 1933. By a well-planned coup he had won the position of Capo or Chief in the Bau Kommando, which placed him at the head of the Construction Division with some four thousand men under his supervision.

The other was Dr. Ernest Busse, also a German, who was the Capo of the hospitals. He exploited this position to its fullest for the benefit of the prisoners. Many times a prisoner would ask Emil, "When will the war end?"

Emil always had the same answer. "As long as you can still see one SS soldier, the war is still on."

Other than this cryptic remark he never spoke about the war, never discussed politics or expressed an opinion even in the most confidential circles. He carried out his duties with the most uncompromising integrity and dignity. And he saved lives.

But we did not need Emil to tell us about the war.

We were quite well informed since the loudspeaker announced the news three times each day. We knew how to discount the German presentation of developments and arrive at some fairly accurate estimate of the truth. We knew what it meant when the loud-speaker blared, "We retired, for strategic reasons, to previously prepared positions."

We knew the Red Army was advancing. We knew that the number of "previously prepared positions" between Stalingrad and Berlin must sooner or later come to an end.

20

The day after we first met Emil he took us to the Office of Workers' Statistics where clerks made a record of each prisoner's civilian occupation. Of the sixty prisoners who worked in that office, about forty-five were reliable "politicals" who played an important rale in the life of the camp. From the prisoners' standpoint the interview in the Office of Statistics was a matter of life or death. Nazis picked workers on the basis of these interviews, and their choice of assignment was vital. It was possible to stay alive on some Buchenwald jobs. On others it was not.

We had our first glimpse of Emil at work. He pointed out to the clerks that most of our group were skilled men, cabinet makers, tailors, tool-and-die makers, shoemakers. Formerly this would have been meaningless since Jews were automatically assigned unskilled labor. But the outlook had improved.

Trained men among us might possibly work in the factories or shops, but first we would have to labor on construction jobs to prove ourselves tough and trustworthy.

After our visit to the Office of Statistics, we waited for the remaining series of injections. Usually this was completed in a week's time. But Emil, together with the doctor at the injection clinic, arranged matters so that five weeks passed and we still had not finished our course of injections. The others in our Block wondered why we were still idle. Never before had anyone in good health spent five weeks in the Big Lager without working.

Emil's arrangement was a gamble. He wanted to gain time for us so that as soon as skilled work became available for Jews we would go straight into the shops. If we were first assigned laborer's work it was a foregone conclusion that the brutal supervisors would finish some of us off before we changed jobs.

Finally Emil could delay no longer. Our injections were incomplete, but an order from the Workers' Statistics Office came through, assigning us to jobs the following morning. We were sent to Bau Kommando No. 3, one of the best of the outside jobs. The same evening we each received a long zebra striped overcoat, unlined, and not very warm, but Emil had managed to retrieve the warm underclothing which we had surrendered on our arrival, as well as our shaving material, shirts, socks, rubbers, and other odds and ends that would make life more comfortable. We had enough clothing now to withstand the twenty-degree temperature on the outside jobs. After we had sewn the prison numbers and Jewish stars to the striped atrocities that passed for overcoats, Emil called us together and delivered an official speech, in the hearing of the old-timers.

"All of you have rested sufficiently by now to set to work. Remember that Buchenwald is no rest home. If there were some sort of system at that injection clinic you would have been at work long ago. Once more I warn you—do your full share on the job."

Our five weeks leisure was at an end, but during that time our group of political prisoners had established friendly relations with the others.

We even succeeded in shaking them out of their deathly lethargy. Now when their packages arrived they shared them with us as well as with the boys, using Emil as a go-between.

We were doing our best to share in the responsibilities of Buchenwald life. By being very strict about cleanliness we held at bay the infectious diseases that decimated the population of the Small Lager, a few hundred meters away. Every week we sent our underwear to the camp steam laundry, and every week we took a shower. Every two weeks there was a louse-examination, and although this robbed us of three hours' sleep, we allowed no absentees. On Wednesdays and Saturdays two health inspectors supervised a physical examination after evening

Appel. This kept us up long past midnight. SS men had no hand in these hygienic measures. They were entrusted entirely to the prisoners' own officials. The only contribution the SS made to our well-being was the sign over each barracks door: "Eine Laus, deine Tod." (One louse may be your death.)

Christmas of 1943 fell during this five weeks of idleness in the barracks, and we prisoners received a treat in the purest of Nazi spirits. We had hoped that out of respect for the holiday we would be spared evening Appel, or at any rate it would be cut short. We still had something to learn of the fascist mentality because it turned out to be the most excruciating Appel we ever experienced.

Christmas night was the coldest night of the winter of 1943. Even the most warmly dressed of us were on the verge of collapse from cold. Steam formed by our breathing froze on our upper lips and in the rim of our nostrils. We took our places at half past six in the evening, and by eight o'clock, when the counting finally began, even our stomachs were icy inside of us.

And then the worst happened. A man was missing. When a man was missing at Appel it could mean only one thing: the SS would have to count over again. It is no brief matter to count twenty-five thousand under any conditions, even when a hundred men do the counting. After nine o'clock the second count revealed the same discrepancy:

one man missing. By ten o'clock, after three and a half hours, of standing at attention in the cold, the loud-speaker was still blaring away, calling the absent man's name and number which the SS had determined by then. Meanwhile the camp Schuttzes—a whole army of SS troopers—were turning the barracks inside out to find the missing man. He was not in his own barracks. They searched all the others.

They poked into every imaginable hiding place. We wondered who he was and we swore that if ever we got our hands on him, we would beat the life out of him without mercy. And we would have done it. Remaining away from Appel was the deadliest crime a prisoner could commit against his fellows. Proof of it was the growing heap of the dead.

Then the SS officer announced via the loudspeaker that Appel would continue until they found the absentee, even if it took three days and three nights. Our curses followed the absent man, wherever he might be. One thing was certain: he would never survive the night.

Eleven o'clock. The hunt went on.

At half past eleven two SS soldiers finally reported that they had found him. Sometime during the afternoon the poor exhausted creature had fallen asleep in an obscure corner of the place where he worked, and there he had frozen to death. He was stiff as a stone when the SS men picked him up.

In this manner the Nazis celebrated Christ's birthday. By the time we returned to the Block it was midnight. We did not work the next day (a Christmas present!) but we had to get up at four in the morning for the usual morning Appel.

On New Year's Day, 1944, we worked only until noon, as on Sundays. New Year's fell on a Saturday. On all half-days, Sundays, and special holidays, Appel began at two in the afternoon. We lined up in the courtyard. No officials were present. The SS men in charge of the count were sleeping off a New Year's Eve celebration, and they were in no hurry to get out of bed. We stood there in the cold and waited, and waited. Still no one came. We could not leave or break ranks. The guards, looking down from their comfortably heated turrets, smiled in good spirits as they watched prisoner after prisoner fall to the ground.

At five o'clock that afternoon the celebrants finally arrived and began to count us. We were all there—except for the one hundred and ten men who had died that afternoon for the sake of a few degenerates with hangovers.

Since we only worked a half day on New Year's, we had to work a full day on January second, even though it was a Sunday. Yet it was better to work twelve hours than stand three hours at Appel.

A man had a better chance of surviving work.

21

One day in Buchenwald I managed to have a few minutes conversation with a young Gentile Hungarian from another Block. His name was Bela Kondas, and he was typical of a small Hungarian landowner's son. His father was wealthy, as wealthy as a small Hungarian landowner could be. He owned two hundred acres, two farmhouses, ten horses, a hundred head of cattle, all of which represented a sizable fortune in a poverty-stricken land.

Bela was an only son, and there would have been no trouble in the Kondas household had he not lost his head and married a Jewish girl. This happened when the Szallasy gang in Hungary was still a little subdued in its worship of Hitler, and had as yet no influence in the government. Bela's marriage violated no laws, and by the time the Szallasy gang took power he was the father of a six-year-old daughter.

Bela Kondas did not live on the farm with his father, but in the capital where he worked at his profession as an engineer. He soon realized he would have to hide his wife and child to conceal them from the Hungarian Nazis. The time came when Jews could not show themselves on the Budapest streets unless they wore the yellow star. Bela took his family to his father's estate and begged the old man to give them sanctuary.

Bela Kondas told me all this, word for word, as we found a few moments to talk together in Buchenwald.

"What did the old man say?" I asked.

"First he grumbled. He said, 'I told you not to marry a Jewish girl, didn't I?' And so on. But he couldn't refuse me. He took my wife and child and they lived there peacefully enough for a month or two. Then I got a letter. My wife wrote me to come and take them away. My father didn't want them any longer. He was afraid."

"What was he afraid of?" (As if I didn't know!)

"The Nazis announced that if they found anyone sheltering Jews they'd confiscate all his money and subject him to the Jewish laws, too." Bela was silent for a few minutes and I did not intrude on his thoughts. Then he continued. "I rushed down to my father's farm. He told me—he was very sharp about it—he told me he couldn't keep my family under his roof any more. He couldn't risk his possessions, his own life.

I said all right, I'd take my wife and child away. But I told him that when the time came, I'd go along with them to the death camp."

"What did he say to that?"

"He said, 'That's your affair, not mine.'"

I could understand that a selfish old man would not protect his daughter-in-law at the risk of his fortune, but it was hard to believe that he would send a grandchild to certain death. But that's what happened.

Inevitably the Nazis caught up with Bela's wife and child. Bela kept his promise. He went along with them. He thought they would all go to the same camp where he might protect and care for them, but that was not the Nazi system. A young mother and a young child could have only one destination: an extermination camp in Poland. But since Bela was capable of hard labor he ended up in Buchenwald.

I saw him many times during our imprisonment, and he was always the same, always mourning his wife and child. Once I said to him, "What will you do if we ever get out of Buchenwald?"

He did not hesitate. "I'm going back to my father's farm," he said. "And I hope, for his sake, that I don't find him alive when I get there."

22

Among the group of sixty prisoners who had arrived ten days before us was a man named Bloch, who was about seventy-five years old, and his son of forty. They were Hungarians who had lived in Berlin for many years. Nazis had dragged father, mother, and son from their Berlin apartment and put them in a near-by concentration camp. Then the mother went to Ravensbruck and the father and son to Buchenwald.

I had many conversations with the two Blochs during the few weeks we were there together. They were pleasant, cultured people. The old man had been head of an architect's office, and the son was both an architectural engineer, and a painter. The younger Bloch was a sensitive and gentle soul, but he was also rather pampered. It was obvious from his dependence upon his parents that he had never married. He worried constantly about his mother, and he watched over the elder Bloch so closely that his father might have been a babe in arms.

The younger Bloch had a right to worry. He knew very well what awaited the older prisoners if they could not meet the requirements of work. After all, the old Hungarian who had first spoken to us, the man who had injured his leg, had disappeared in the last few days, and everyone knew better than to ask questions. There was a certain injection used in such cases, merely a scratch, no more, but it did its work in a minute. Perhaps the elder Bloch did not realize his danger.

There was trouble the very first day we went to work. The old man hadn't the strength to break the earth with his pick. Young Bloch, seeing his father's difficulties, tried to do his work for him, as well as his own. He dug frantically at the excavation assigned his father. But an able-bodied man had all he could do to keep up with his own work, and this architect-engineer, who was not used to manual labor, could not survive this double task for long.

Then one of the supervisors noticed what was happening. He gave the old man a terrible beating for allowing his son to help. Then he gave a similar beating to young Bloch for helping his father. (The beatings were unofficial.)

Young Bloch stood up under the beating, but the old man was so severely injured that the prisoners had to carry him back to the barracks. The son continued working. When he returned to the Block that night he couldn't find his father. The supervisor had reported the case to the hospital.

The next day, as we all expected, the hospital sent a message to the Jewish Block, informing us that the old man was dead. To add to his sorrow, young Bloch received word on the same day that his mother had died in Ravensbruck.

His mother and father—just about the only two people for whom he really cared! He sobbed quietly at the table as we ate our carrot soup and scraps of leftover bread. We tried to console him, but what could console a man in Buchenwald where everyone was in need of consolation?

I walked over to him and patted his shoulder, trying with the clumsy words that come to hand on such occasions to express my sympathy.

He murmured, "Thank you, thank you."

Emil, too, approached him and said quietly, "We mustn't break down, Bloch. We have to be able to face anything here."

"I can't help it."

He continued to mourn quietly so as not to disturb others, and he was considerate and well-mannered in his grief as in all things. Then he went to bed, throwing himself down in his bunk with his clothes on.

A little after midnight the man who shared the bunk with Bloch crept out, slipped over to one of the room attendants, and woke him up.

"What's wrong?" asked the attendant.

The other sat on the edge of the bunk and whispered. "It's Bloch," he said. "He's all excited. He's mumbling. He swears that he's going to get revenge in the morning. He says he's going to take his pick and break open some SS guard's head first chance he gets at work. He doesn't give a damn if they kill him or not."

"He said that?"

"Yes. I thought I'd better tell you. He might do it. The man's half crazy."

"All right. Go on back. We'll take care of it."

The situation was dynamite for the entire Jewish Block. Not long before an "Aryan" political prisoner had cut a factory belt out of an uncontrollable desire to sabotage the enemy. It did not take long for guards to discover the cut. They immediately lined up all the men who worked in the vicinity of the belt, and machine-gunned them. The damaged belt cost two hundred human lives! It was easy to imagine what might happen if a Jew performed an act, not of sabotage, but of violence against a German in the service of the Fuehrer. How many of the four hundred Jews in Block 22 would be left alive?

Perhaps Bloch did not understand this, but Emil, the attendants, and the old-timers knew it only too well. Bloch didn't even have to commit any overt act. If the Germans got wind of his words, of the mere threat, that alone would be enough to stimulate a massacre.

Emil soon came in and spoke to the attendant.

"What's Bloch's condition now?" he asked.

"I tried to quiet him, but it's no use. He's in a bad way."

"Would it do any good if I spoke to him?"

The attendant shrugged doubtfully. "He wants to die anyway."

"Do you think he'd do it?"

"I don't know. Maybe not. Maybe he'll calm down."

Maybe.

Can the lives of four hundred men depend on a "maybe"? If Bloch himself were to swear that he wouldn't carry out his threat, could we place trust in the word of a man no longer responsible for his actions? Could our leaders endanger the lives in their care and open the door to Nazi machine-guns?

Emil went to Bloch's side. He spoke quietly to the grieving man, trying to soothe him to instill some hope, describing how his own family had been killed, how all of us in the Block had lost our families in the gas chambers, by machine-gun fire or overwork. Yet we continued to carry on. Emil warned him that any action against an SS man might mean the death of all of us.

Bloch refused to listen. If we wanted to go on living this way, it was our affair. He knew what he wanted to do and he was going to do it.

If Bloch went to morning Appel he might talk in the same vein. SS men might hear. He might make some foolhardy gesture, or lose control of himself in some other way.

Before the Appel whistle, the hospital sent for Bloch.

We never saw him again.

23

Nobody ever forgets his first day of work in Buchenwald.

Before the war I earned my living as a carpenter. From the day I hammered my first nail, I enjoyed my trade. I set out for my shop each morning with pleasant anticipation. Work brought me bread and respect, but even more important, it made my life complete and reasonable.

Yet on January 19, 1944, I faced work with the deepest fear and uncertainty. I was setting out to do slave labor, work that would serve to strengthen a shameful and dishonorable enemy. And I was doomed because my masters would take from me ten times the energy they were willing to replace in the form of food.

The only cheering aspect was that others, my comrades and friends, stood by my side as we waited. The Capos and supervisors lined us up in fives to count us. The Capo of our group bared his head and reported to the SS man on guard. The SS man sported a swagger stick with which he counted us again, making a note of our number. In the evening he would have to account for the same number, dead or alive. As he counted the Buchenwald band stood nearby and played German marches.

We were only a small segment of the sixteen hundred men who labored daily in Buchenwald. The SS guard led us on our way, and we walked for twenty minutes before we reached an enormous building, almost completed. We had arrived at Bau Kommando No. 1, the building division, relatively the best of all the work Kommandos.

The Capos released groups of men to various overseers. As a new group, we stayed in a separate line. We no longer numbered sixty-nine, but only fifty-eight, since eleven of us had already died. The Capo made another speech, brief and loud. He told us what our responsibilities would be. He, too, declared that the Nazis would demand more of the Jews than the other prisoners, but the Capo was a truth worthy "political," and we knew he was putting on an act for the Nazis. Emil's influence reached here, too.

Then the Capo assigned us to an overseer who turned out to be a very decent sort. He immediately sent the young boys to work in a warm and sheltered spot, and he showed genuine consideration for us by assigning the older men to lighter duties. Everywhere we felt the friendly touch of Emil's hand.

My friend Sapir drew light duty, but since I was in good physical condition, my assignment was a hard one. I had to carry fifty kilogram sacks of cement a distance of a hundred meters from the store-house to the building. I was equal to the job, but working with us were weaker men who grew exhausted after a few trips. The younger of us, myself included, pitched in to help them. We had agreed among our group that we would help one another to whatever extent was possible, rather than surrender to the dog-eat-dog philosophy which poisoned the minds of some prisoners.

The building on which we worked was one of a group of twelve huge factory units, five of which were already completed and in operation. The largest of these was the Gustlov Gun Factory which produced heavy artillery and lighter weapons. The other plants produced munitions, gas, and similar war materials. Several thousand men worked in each of these factories, both prisoners and civilian employees.

The buildings under construction were planned on a still larger scale. Nearby was a half-completed tool factory designed to employ twelve hundred workers. Crates of equipment were already there, giant machines which the Nazis had stolen from conquered countries throughout Europe. This was the year 1944, and the Germans still believed that efficient factories, looted machinery, and slave labor would win the war for them. Even the advances of the Red Army did not yet weaken their faith in their own strength, and they never dreamed that an American or British bomb might demolish in a few moments all these gigantic structures. They thieved; they looted. We saw French machines, machines from the Skoda works in Czechoslovakia, power engines stamped with the names of factories stretching from the Dniester to the Belgian coast. Using stolen energy, my energy, the energy of my imprisoned friends, they continued to build with the sweat of others, with a man's last spasm of muscular energy forced from him under the lash. The self-assurance and maniacal egotism of German plans were amazing and frightening.

Prisoner-engineers designed the factories. Skilled inmates built them. We learned that our work would at least have the saving grace of variety. In the days to come we would do various jobs, sometimes carrying cement, sometimes mixing mortar or carting bricks. And whenever the mood stirred them into action, the SS soldiers would beat us for alleged laziness or misdemeanors, or for helping each other.

Coal earned us some of our beatings. It was generally so cold that the stone-masons couldn't work without a little fire in an iron pail somewhere on the wall nearby or upon their scaffolding. The SS men did not object to this. We, who did not work on the walls or scaffolding, usually kept a few pieces of coal glowing in an iron pot over which we warmed our fingers now and then. The coal was scattered all about on the ground.

Buchenwald had inexplicable rules. The SS men never questioned us if they saw the coal burning in the pot—but if they caught anyone picking up a piece they beat him without mercy. It was against regulations to build a fire but they permitted us to keep a fire. They yielded to the accomplished fact.

I witnessed a typical "unofficial" beating on the first day of work. A Hungarian baker from Berlin, a recent arrival at Buchenwald, was a little near-sighted and didn't see the SS trooper when he stooped to pick up a piece of coal for his fire-pot. The guard immediately gave him a frightful beating. He had almost finished hitting the poor man when he noticed the Jewish emblem on the victim's sweater.

That gave the guard new energy. With purely animal rage, he pulled off all the baker's upper garments and tore them to shreds, and then whipped his bare back until the blood oozed through the abased skin. The baker sank to the ground in a semi-conscious state. Then the overseer, a Czech-German "political," noticed what was going on. He immediately rushed over and began shouting, "You god-damn Jewish dog! You'll work for the rest of the day without clothes! I'm sick of the trouble you lousy Jews give me!" He made a threatening gesture, and then roared, "Come with me!"

The SS guard left, confident that the baker was in good hands. Then the overseer took the baker into a toolshed where it was warm, dressed him, washed his wounds, and gave him permission to stay in the shed until it was time to quit work.

Unfortunately the affair did not end there. The guard had made note of the baker's number, which meant that when the day was ended and Appel finally done, he would be sent out to work all night as punishment. Night work multiplied the tortures of the day a thousand-fold. There was, for instance, the threat of the quarry. The Germans sent robbers and murderers to the quarry, men who had committed crimes on their own initiative rather than under official orders. The average life of a prisoner who broke rocks in the quarry was two weeks, if he happened to be built like an ox.

Our baker did not go to the quarry. They had reserved for him a still more delicate assignment:

the pit, ten meters deep, in which human excrement was collected. Every three weeks thirty prisoners emptied this pit, carrying the fecal matter in pails to the vegetable garden, a distance of sixty meters. They lowered the pails, filled them, drew them up, and made the trip, repeating this process all night long.

The location was slippery and unlighted. Of the thirty men on this assignment, an average of ten fell into the pit in the course of each night's work. The others were not allowed to pull the victims out.

When work was done and the pit empty, then and then only were they permitted to remove the corpses.

I learned these lessons on my first day at work in Buchenwald. But I also learned that the spirit which we in the Belgian Resistance called "Solidarity," lived even in these surroundings. There is an indestructible something called human dignity, and no matter how degraded some of the German people became, they discovered that there were always men who could not be reduced to their level.

24

The baker returned at two that morning from the excrement pit, in wretched condition. We had clean clothes and underwear ready for him; the attendant and his bunkmate gave him a bath and laid him down to sleep for the remaining two hours of the night. While he slept we washed his dirty clothes and put them away to be used as spares. We did not have the energy for the work, but we had the magic of solidarity.

The months passed. In February a new transport arrived bringing, among others, forty-five Jews from Holland. The Jewish Block now had four hundred inmates, including three rabbis, several doctors, engineers, merchants, and even a few industrialists.

One of the new group was a Dr. Frieder who had been an active Resistance fighter before his arrest in The Hague. Dr. Frieder became a stonemason's helper. He was an incorrigible optimist, and after his twelve hours of work he became the doctor for the barracks. He gave advice, bandaged wounds, and cheered the despondent. If help was needed, there he was! Nobody knew how it came about, but a few days after his arrival he had on hand a stock of aspirin and bandages to aid him in his work. The others in his group also added to the morale of Block 22 because they were "politicals," veterans of the Resistance.

The most striking of them was a young Hungarian from Holland named Perlmutter, a man about twenty-eight years old. He had the build of a trained athlete. He was six feet tall, handsome, perfectly proportioned, all muscle. Perlmutter was with us ten days when he received the order to report to Block 51. He started out happily enough because he wouldn't have to spend the day carrying sacks of cement. We did not tell him that Block 51 was the Experimental Station. He would discover that soon enough.

Two weeks later Emil received instructions to take Perlmutter's name off the list of inmates in our Block. That was all.

Nazi "doctors" must have learned much from Perlmutter's splendid physique. How long, I wonder, did his heart beat when they laid it on the table? And today I also wonder how many of those German "doctors" the Allies have hanged. I have followed the news closely but I have heard of only two so far.

After Perlmutter's disappearance the Workers' Statistical Office sent through the notice for which we were all hoping. Three men from our Block might go to work in the Carpenter Shop. Only three —as a test. Emil chose me, a Hungarian boy from Strassburg, and an old Antwerp acquaintance of mine. Ours was a great responsibility. If we met the test there was a chance for all the other skilled Jews. Emil called the three of us together after Appel, and urged us to do our very best. "I recommended you because I have confidence in you. You've got to pass muster."

The shop, which employed twelve hundred carpenters, cabinetmakers, coopers, and wheelwrights, was equipped with the most modern machinery, stolen by the most modern methods. It was almost a factory rather than a shop. The workers produced building parts and furniture for the apartments of the SS officers.

For us three newcomers the shop was a tremendous improvement. Immediately following morning Appel we went to work in a well-heated and comfortable building. A skilled SS man tested us out. We passed the test. We were there to stay.

Apart from the constant hunger pangs our life in the shop was bearable. We didn't work on Sundays. Like all other enterprises in and about the camp, the shop was a privately owned business (more "National Socialism"). Technically we received wages, but our wages went to the administrative heads of the camp as payment for our keep. The private owners paid 800 to 1000 marks a week for each prisoner's services, plus an additional sum for our daily rations. I can imagine what the camp authorities charged for the half-liter of coffee, the liter of soup, and the fist-sized lump of black bread.

We received three marks a week for ourselves. These were camp marks, good only at the Buchenwald canteen where we might buy a little bad-smelling cabbage or a pint of poor beer. But we were treated quite well on the job, and it was important that we did not work outside in the freezing weather.

Then I had the greatest stroke of luck possible. The supervisor assigned me to the night shift, the best of all assignments. The night shift men worked from six in the evening to six in the morning, and did not have to stand Appel. Guards counted us in the shop.

Furthermore, when we returned from work in the morning the barracks were almost vacant except for a few convalescents and the attendants. After we swallowed our black bread and coffee ration, we could sleep undisturbed, each man with a bunk to himself! We could have slept until five in the afternoon if we wished, but we usually rose at three to read the papers and listen to the news broadcasts.

Yet we had some difficulties in the shop, the same difficulties which Emil had met when he first arrived. There was conflict, particularly among the newcomers, about the best way for prisoners to conduct themselves. Some favored sabotage, others shared Emil's view, and still others spoke for a slow-down of production. The Russian and Czech prisoners-of-war were all advocates of the latter, but our supervisor, a veteran "political," warned us to steer clear of any such approach. The Ukrainian White Guardists were constantly trying to lead us into acts of sabotage, and I am convinced that these attempts were definite provocations.

I worked with a small circular saw, and my helper was a Ukrainian. My two companions were given the same work. One had a Russian helper, the other a Pole. The Ukrainian and the Pole were forever watching for an opportunity to destroy one of the machines. I tried to explain to the Ukrainian that the machine would be out of commission for half an hour at most, while any number of prisoners would be dead—permanently. He and the Pole were a constant menace to the safety of the prisoners. And finally, to crown my difficulties, one of the SS men, a Rumanian who spoke Hungarian, persisted, despite all the rules, in standing by my side and talking to me for hours on end. He was not a vicious man, but what he lacked in brutality, he made up in stupidity.

He could have got us in plenty of trouble for these casual conversations. And the other workers began to eye me queerly, since it was no common thing for a Jewish prisoner to chat with an SS man.

Finally I asked the supervisor to change my helper, which he did. Later I discovered that the Jewish star on my jacket inspired the Ukrainian to try to make trouble for me.

My morale and that of the men working with me was at a new high despite the disagreements as to procedure in the shop. The major reason for the change in our spirits were the American and British bombing raids which were now regular occurrences.

Neither we nor the Nazis expected Buchenwald to be bombed. The Allies knew their own friends populated the camps, and we thought there was little likelihood that they would bomb unfinished factories when there were so many more desirable targets.

Consequently we ignored daytime air-raid sirens. If, however, the siren sounded at night, we had to go to the basement where we would stay for a few hours until the all-clear. While we were in the shelter we smoked the fifteen cigarettes allotted the factory workers. Then we had to make up the lost time by working extra hours, although we could have finished in four hours the work assigned us for twelve.

From time to time I reported to Emil on our progress in the shop, and he was satisfied. The days passed. The Russians were now well within Poland and prisoners arriving from the West told of the frantic Nazi terror in Holland and France. The advance of the Red Army evidently inspired the Nazis to new bestiality. In the beginning of March a transport containing two thousand French partisans arrived in Buchenwald after a journey of three days.

While still on French soil they had attempted a break for freedom. The Germans retaliated by stripping everybody in the group to the skin and locking their clothes in a separate freight car. The French had traveled three days in the deadly cold, completely naked, locked in the freight cars. I say a transport of two thousand, but that is the original figure. Only sixteen hundred reached Buchenwald alive, and of these, about five hundred died in the next month.

Large and small groups from Holland and Belgium also poured into the camp. The Germans were preparing for the Second Front. They were clearing out all dangerous people from the coastal areas, and those who were neither Nazis nor quislings were dangerous.

All the newcomers were in desperate need of underclothing and food. Our job was to collect these necessities out of nowhere. We had to gather them from the most naked, poverty-stricken, hungry crowd of men on the face of the earth in order to provide for those who had even less. But we managed. Packages were turned over intact to the newcomers. We collected shreds and scraps, and somehow made them do service.

The French and Belgians immediately formed their own Solidarity organization during the first week, and we Hungarians from the West joined forces with them. This movement gave a tremendous impetus to the morale of the entire camp. It soon involved the Russians, Czechs, and later the Poles, and Germans. Now we had members of our Solidarity working in the kitchen, and they managed at times to produce a hundred liters of soup for new prisoners near death.

It was March. Curiously enough each single day was slow, tortuous, but the weeks sped by. We spent March waiting for the Hungarians. The radio announcer, to the background of the usual musical flourishes, had announced that the German Army had occupied Hungary. We knew that following such an occupation another army in chains, an army of Jews and left-wingers who were still alive, would soon be on its way to Buchenwald. Huge numbers of Czech and Austrian Jews arrived first, however, and they gave us information about events in Hungary following the German occupation and the establishment of the Szallasy regime.

Changes occurred in my own life. I was transferred back to the day shift which again made Appel obligatory for me. Once more I had to share my narrow bunk with a companion. Day workers, however, received slightly more to eat. I was lucky again in that I was assigned the job of washing the soup containers. This enabled me to get three or four extra liters of soup for a few seriously ailing men who waited up for me in the evening.

My shop assignment was now in the gluing department. More Jews were employed in the skilled jobs, and I had a young Czech-Jewish helper. He represented a battle won. The helper, whose name was Peter, was about twenty-four years old, skillful, clever, tall but painfully emaciated from ten months spent in Auschwitz. He was one of those who reversed the usual procedure and came in a transport from Auschwitz to Buchenwald.

The Nazis had employed Peter, who was a gentle and friendly boy, as a human butcher.

25

The second day of my new job the air-raid siren sounded. We were ordered not to ignore it and to take shelter in the cellar. I sat there next to Peter for about three hours while we smoked and talked.

"Tell me about Auschwitz," I began. "Did you work there?"

"Yes. But not this kind of work."

"What did you do?"

"Oh, the young fellows got all sorts of jobs. I worked with six other people in the gas chambers for a couple of months."

He said it almost casually. "The gas chambers?"

I was astounded. He seemed so calm. "What did you do there?"

"Well, not very much. I just helped guide people in. In six weeks the seven of us led eighteen thousand people into the gas chambers."

Peter might as well have been telling me that he and six friends tended eighteen sheep in the fields. I could detect no emotion, no excitement in his drawn face. I knew he was telling me the truth but something inside me insisted that it was a lie.

Peter spoke on, calmly as ever. "The young men who worked at the gas chambers were executed after two or three months on the job. They don't want witnesses. But they didn't put us in the chambers. They knew they'd have one hell of a job getting us in there. They used machine-guns or the needle." He looked at me and saw that I was surprised that he was alive. He smiled. "We knew the routine, you see. We managed to outsmart them."

Suddenly I doubted the whole story. He was a young fellow with imagination, indulging in some kind of perverse boasting, trying to impress me with his cleverness. Right out from under the noses of the Nazis! I smiled. He caught the smile, recognized it as expressing disbelief, and continued in an impersonal tone.

"It wasn't much of a trick. They assigned a lot of dead people to the transports. They never knew who was dead, who was alive. We picked out a few dead ones and changed their numbers for our own. Then we reported to the proper transport. We didn't care where they took us so long as it was far away from Auschwitz. That's how I got here. There are three other fellows here right now who worked with me in Auschwitz."

He was clearly implying that he had witnesses if I chose to doubt his story, but the remark was unnecessary. I had ceased doubting.

From far above we could distinguish the thundering of anti-aircraft guns and the dull muffled explosion of distant bombs. We went on talking.

"Look," Peter explained, "we knew they'd keep us there three months at the most. So we got away ahead of time. The supervision over individuals isn't too strict in Auschwitz. It's almost impossible in a place where they kill thousands every day. They can't check on everyone. Our lives were worth just as much as anyone else's, no more." His eyes clouded and then he murmured, irrelevantly, as though he were reminiscing, "They used to give them each a piece of soap and a towel."

Buchenwald does strange things to a man. My next question was not about the people. I asked, "Real soap?" It seemed incredible that the Nazis, would waste a precious item like real soap in such a fashion.

"Of course not. The stuff just looked like soap. Then they came toward us. Old people, women, children. No young men. There were a lot of young mothers, or just young women."

I must have shuddered because he looked at me curiously. I understood again what I had seen in other prisoners. Peter was neither hard nor calloused. He had simply adopted this cold and objective approach to save himself from hopeless insanity.

He sympathized with my revulsion because he asked, appeasingly, "Shall I go on or have you had enough?"

"Never mind, go on," I said, wondering if scientists would ever devise a term to denote people who have sunk to the level of Nazis in the year 1944.

"Some people don't like to hear these things. Most of us don't talk about them. We make believe it never happened, but we know better." He paused for a while, seeking the thread of thought where he had dropped it. "All the people came toward us with the towels and soap as though they were going to the showers."

"Didn't they suspect?" I asked. "The Germans have been killing people that way for a long time. Didn't they know they were going to their deaths?"

"I used to wonder about that myself," Peter said.

"But it seems most of them didn't suspect anything.

They came along quietly. I only heard of one occasion when they realized what was happening and refused to enter the gas chamber."

"When?"

"In 1942. One of the group that worked with me told me about it. Two hundred Greek prisoners were on their way to the gas chambers. They found out where they were going. The Greek Jews rebelled. They wouldn't go in. The SS officer on duty whistled for troopers, and they turned machine-guns on the crowd. The Greeks knew they were going to die anyway, but I guess they preferred the bullets to the gas. They couldn't do much, but they charged the SS men. The machineguns cut them down pretty quickly, killed almost all, but some of them were only wounded. Then the Nazis threw them into the cremating ovens, the wounded and the dead all together. It's the only case like that I ever heard of. Most of the groups went peacefully enough because they didn't know where they were going. Or maybe they didn't care by that time. We had from eighty to one hundred and twenty people in a group.

They came in on trucks and they went to the chambers without a word. Our job was to bolt the doors on them and to shut the air vents. You see, they leave the air vents open between executions to air out the place. When the victims get inside, they stand there, waiting for the water to be turned on. Then an SS soldier turns on the gas. Gas rises, you know, so the little children close to the floor don't get it as quickly as the adults. They stay alive long after their mothers, but they're unconscious.

The Nazis give them six minutes, and then they take the whole group to the crematorium. Most are dead. Some are just unconscious. In half an hour the whole business is finished. Then we opened the air vents. We usually waited about two hours before the trucks arrived with the next batch, all supplied with soap and towels."

I sat there hypnotized by Peter's dispassionate recital, and I know I felt a little faint. "But Peter,

I said, "Once they were inside the gas chamber didn't they realize what was happening?"

"Sure they did. But it was too late. They buried their nails in each other's backs, trying to get to the door. But they were packed in so tightly they couldn't move backward or forward. Most of them didn't even fall down. They just died like that, standing on their feet, pressed together, while the children suffocated under their feet. I heard them scream once in a while. The screams were awful but we usually couldn't hear because the band played loud marches." He took a deep breath. Evidently this recital, little as his voice betrayed any emotion, was rapidly tiring him. "The gas chamber wasn't in Auschwitz," he explained. "It was at Birkenau, about two kilometers away. Auschwitz itself was a work camp something like this, but a lot larger."

He spoke in a very low voice now, and I could see he wanted to stop talking about the gas chambers. But I was still curious about one point.

"Tell me, Peter," I said, "why did you agree to do the job?"

Peter looked at me a long time. He was deep in thought. I could see that he had never fully resolved the answer to that question in his own mind. Then he said, in a steady voice, "They killed everyone who refused. I wouldn't be saving anyone's life if I refused. I'd only be adding my own death to the others. There were plenty who refused. The Nazis herded them out, made them dig their own graves, and then shot them right at the edge of the grave. Sometimes they even threw them into the graves first and shot them there."

"Why didn't they resist while they were digging the graves? What was there to lose?"

"Why? Because they still had a few minutes of life left. I think those few minutes represented hope to them. Who can tell?"

26

Allied bombing flights increased in number.

There must have been a good many objectives in the immediate neighborhood of Buchenwald. We all became military experts and speculated upon the purpose of those bombing missions. Those of us who had considerable military experience claimed that American bombers were photographing the Camp and the factory buildings in and around it. The Allies knew the factories were close to Buchenwald both because of the proximity of labor power, and the German trust that bombers would not attack concentration camps. That is why the Nazis manufactured the V-ls and V-2s nearby.

We ourselves did not believe that the Allies would bomb the camp, but as planes flew over with purposeful regularity, the theory that they were taking photographs became more logical.

Surely the planes were not using up gasoline for no reason at all. We waited.

Meanwhile two or three new transports arrived every week. As soon as one moved in, another left Buchenwald carrying prisoners to bombed areas to clean away debris and dig out bodies. The use of prisoners for this work was a recent development.

The Germans employed a complicated system of shifting people from camp to camp. Those who arrived at Buchwald were all in the same condition: exhausted, starved, half dead. Each transport arrived with only about two thirds of its original strength. The rest had died en route. This explained the constant shifting of prisoners from camp to camp. The Germans made no secret of the murder of Jews in the gas chambers or elsewhere. Their mentality was so warped that they confidently believed world opinion would accept this without any indignation. But the mass-murder of non-Jews was another matter. They hoped to avoid rousing the Pope's anger as a result of their murder of a million Catholics, and they did riot want to sharpen the opposition of the

Protestant Churches any more than they had already. Therefore the Nazis chose the relatively quiet method of letting prisoners die in transport.

The procedure was for the guards to stuff eighty people into a boarded-up freight car, without food or air. They were packed in too tightly to be down.

The dead—and there were always dead—were accounted for by a report, "Died in transit," or "Shot while attempting to escape." The officials accepted any explanation.

This was the mobile form of execution. Of those who set out on one of these transports, about forty per cent usually died in transit, and of the survivors, almost half were in a dying condition. Those who lived were subjected to another deportation, and another and another. The system worked.

The appearance which these men, women, and children made upon their arrival was fantastic. For days they had stood in freight cars, packed next to each other, with no facilities for relieving themselves. Kultur did not provide water-closets. The air in the cars was unimaginably foul, particularly since standing among the living were the standing dead who soon putrefied. It was not astonishing that so many died. It was astonishing that so many survived.

We could see the arriving transports from the window of the shop where I worked. Frequently a few of us would run out to offer the wretched arrivals a little bit of soup, choosing from the thousands those who seemed at the end of their tether and the children. Sometimes we found youngsters of twelve and thirteen whose parents had declared them to be fifteen in order to save them from the gas chamber. But when we tried to help them the guards drove us away.

Sometimes these newcomers waited in the yard for six or eight hours before using the compulsory showers. Some endured that far and then fell dead, even under the warm water. Many of those who survived the showers went on to be shaved and became hysterical during that ordeal. One Hungarian barber from our group had been assigned to this work. He stuck it out for only three days, and then declared he would rather go to his own death in the quarry. The other barbers often beat the new arrivals to death rather than shave them, since they were so revoltingly filthy. The Hungarian barber told us that he himself had tried to be as considerate as possible, but this aroused the resentment of the other barbers. While he shaved one person, they shaved ten each, and so the greater part of the work fell on their shoulders.

Some time later our prisoner-officials succeeded in improving the situation in the "Haircutting Division" to some extent.

The new prisoners were fed only after the baths and injections. While they stood in the yard they would always beg us for a piece of bread. Compared to them we were splendid physical specimens. We longed to give them bread, but we soon learned not to do so. They were not people when they arrived. None of them was actually in a sane condition. If we gave bread to one or five, the others killed them in a mad scramble for the food. But when the baths and injections were finished the kitchen workers and the Solidarity immediately hurried to take them food.

This mobile system of extermination reflected the stupidity, as well as the brutality, of the German mind at the time. The Wehrmacht needed innumerable soldiers to escort these transports. Thousands of tons of coal which the Germans desperately needed, were burned up in the engines that drew these death trains. And the trains themselves were diverted from the needs of military transportation, delaying the passage of troops and supplies to the fronts. German wounded died because of insufficient transport facilities. The Russians were close to the Prussian frontier, and every German daily paper had at least three pages filled with names of those who had "died a heroic death in the service of the Fuehrer and the Fatherland."

Yet the geniuses of German fascism, in that crucial moment in the fortunes of the German military machine, diverted trains, coal, and military man-power from the fronts and used them in a war against old men, women, and children.

In addition to the transport's mobile form of execution, the Nazis employed a standard stationary form which took place in a yard which we could see from the windows of our workshop. No prisoners were executed there, but only Nazis themselves, or Ukrainian traitors who had joined the SS and had proved themselves unreliable there as well.

There was a fenced-in pit in a remote corner of the yard. From its center rose a wooden stake. The stake was always bloody, and the ground at its base was sprinkled with sawdust. This was the official place of execution by firing squad, an honor reserved for Germans who had committed some offense against the Fuehrer.

As Allied arms pressed forward there were more and more Germans, soldiers and civilians alike, who took a stand against the war in one way or another, deserted the armed forces, spoke disrespectfully of Hitler. These included German soldiers who had grown tired of their honors and of killing, and who became human beings once again; German women who criticized the conduct of the war, or simply wished Hitler in Hell; civilians who lowered Nazi morale or slowed up production.

These prisoners came in vans. A car always followed the van. Six officers stepped from the car and waited for a truck carrying six German soldiers and six Ukrainian SS men. If there was little noise in the shop we would even hear the commands of the officer directing the firing squad.

"Abteilung! Ziel! Feuer!"

All twelve fired at once. They were practised killers. We always heard the shots, and by the time we could look the head of the executed prisoner was bent over, and the body hung limply from the ropes which bound it to the stake. The officers and the squad went back to the vehicles and drove away.

Then two prisoners, who worked in the crematorium, brought a tarpaulin in which they bundled the corpse as though it were a sack of potatoes, and bore it away.

Then came the third man who carried a basket of sawdust. He sprinkled the sawdust over the ground where the blood stained the previous layer. The system never varied.

When an occasional Ukrainian White Guardist was executed, the Russians in the shop would quietly nod their heads, and at times they repeated an old Russian proverb, "God doesn't punish with a stick."

27

In April we were treated to a special radio broadcast on the eve of Hitler's birthday. The loudspeakers roared. The voice of the Fuehrer himself, a guttural, bawling, snarling, wheedling voice, spoke for our edification. Yet we enjoyed the speech because we detected in it a new note. Hitler called for no extended celebrations. He did not prattle, as usual, of the absolute invincibility of Nazism and the German people. Instead he urged everyone to mark the great day by working twice as hard as usual so that the war might sooner reach its victorious conclusion. And then, with no concern for its anti-climactic effect, he explained that the Nazis were retiring on the Russian front in order to concentrate strength in the West where the heroic German Army would annihilate enemy troops when they landed if, indeed, they had the courage to attempt a landing.

"For our bombed cities we will avenge ourselves a hundredfold," said he. "Victory can be ours and ours only."

The next day the camp was hung with a thousand swastika flags. The Fuehrer's face offended us from every corner. There was much official heiling of Hitler, and in the evening the band played songs written in his praise. Meanwhile the Weimar people's courts were sending dozens of condemned Germans every week to our factory courtyard under the escort of the six officers and the twelve SS men. Not everyone worshiped Adolf. The bombings which had devastated Cologne, Frankfurt-am-Main, Berlin, and Munich, were beginning to get on German nerves. They buried their dead by the thousands and the promise of revenge did not console them much.

In May we no longer ignored daytime air-raid alarms. The guards herded us into the barracks, but the SS men rushed into the concrete-lined basements where they believed they would be secure. The planes came every day, but still not one bomb dropped. To the east, west, and north, however, there were plenty of bombs falling, and we could hear their muffled bursts every day. We calculated the distance between our barracks and the war factories, and we wondered if it would be possible for a bomber to hit a target accurately from the height of two thousand meters. We could reach no conclusion.

May first, the labor holiday so widely celebrated in pre-war Europe, was an official holiday of the National Socialist Third Reich. We were given the day off, but like all the prisoners except a handful who had not been arrested for political activity, we boycotted the band music and other celebrations by remaining in the barracks.

On May second a new transport arrived. Through the shop window I could hear the newcomers speaking French and Flemish. I ran out at my first opportunity. As I suspected, the transport had come from Belgium. I found three old friends, co-fighters in the Brussels Resistance, named Riesman, Levay, and B.J. The camp police quickly chased me way, but I shouted that I would come to see them in the evening. I knew they would go to the Small Lager.

I was so anxious to visit my friends that Appel seemed particularly long that night. Emil gave passes to Sapir, to me, and two others, permitting us to visit the Small Lager. We gathered what food we could find, and the men from our Block denied themselves so that we should have more to take to the new prisoners whose need was greater than ours.

When we arrived at the Small Lager we immediately found our friends and talked with them about the work in Belgium. They told us that things were going well, but many of our friends had died since last we were in Antwerp or Brussels. Reisman, Levay, B.J., and the others, had come from the Brenonk concentration camp where they had been sentenced to death, but not executed. The Nazis had brought them to Buchenwald instead, undoubtedly confident that death would find them out in their new home.

Levay told us that our friends heard we had gone to Auschwitz and the gas chambers. Then he recounted how Stephen Molnar, our great Stephen to whom the Belgians have erected a statue, fought his last fight. In an encounter with the Nazis they had shot him six times and then thrown him, still alive, into an automobile, where he bled to death. Levay himself, unharmed, was thrust next to Molnar's side, and then tortured for weeks. Every day the Nazis had performed a make-believe execution by firing squad with Levay as the butt of their grim joke, in an effort to make him give information.

Levay also did me one incalculable service. He brought me news of my son who was in good health. Henri wrote every week to Madame Stephan and she answered his letters. Levay said the child always asked why I didn't write him, but Madame Stephan explained that I was working in France where it was against regulations to correspond.

A few days later the officials broke up this new group. All except Riesman and B.J. were put in the French barracks. Although they were Jews they carried "Aryan" papers and were entered on the books accordingly. The Nazis evidently could not distinguish Jews from the master race unless there were papers to help them. Levay died shortly afterward. Reisman, good "Aryan" that he was, became a guard at one of the entrances to the Small Lagery a circumstance that enabled me and other Hungarians to enter there without a special pass.

Not long afterward more Hungarians arrived en masse. I will never forget that transport. Every transport had affected me deeply, but when I suddenly saw twenty-five hundred of, my countrymen, ragged, dirty, hungry, speaking my language as they stood in the yard, I could not hold back the tears. There they stood in rows of five, their ranks disciplined, the yellow triangle on their chests and the large letter "U." This was the largest group ever to arrive at one time. I ran to the fence, where others already stood, and called out to them in my native tongue, "Are you Hungarians?" I knew that they were, but I wanted to identify myself.

All eyes turned to me, the compatriot, and suddenly hundreds of voices asked the same dread question. "Is there a gas chamber in Buchenwald, too?"

They had come in a transport from Auschwitz and life, therefore, was a miracle. I tried to put their minds at rest with a word of cheer. "Don't be afraid. There's no gas chamber. It won't be so bad here."

A stone struck me on the head. One of the prisoner-policemen had thrown it as a polite hint that I move quickly and stop breaking regulations. I hurried off, a little dizzy from the blow.

Later ray two Hungarian companions and I in the Block set out to collect food for twenty-five hundred men. We went from barracks to barracks, asking for soup and bread. In my own barracks we were getting repeta, as the extra half-liter of soup distributed twice weekly was called. In the workshop thirty of the forty-two men in my department gave us their liter and a half of soup, and the rest offered their repeta. German and Czech politicals who worked on the ambulances contributed fifteen liters.

Others brought in small amounts. The Czech cook gave us twenty-five kilograms of bread and fifty liters of soup because Emil came with us to the kitchen. The twenty-five hundred newcomers were each scheduled to receive the official half-liter of soup, and nothing more till the next day when they would have the regular bread and soup ration.

We estimated how far the food we had collected would go and decided to give most of it to the more ailing of the prisoners who had been segregated in Number 4 Tent. When we entered with our donation I was happy to see that our Belgian friends were already waiting with gifts of bread and soup. There were four hundred and thirty men in the tent, all almost dead of starvation. (Three, in fact, had already died.) Two attendants distributed the food in equal portions among them. Emil supervised. All their physical and mental resistance at an end, the prisoners cried and babbled like small children.

It was the usual story. In the Austrian camp where they had been held a few days, they had met the standard animal brutality of the Nazis. Their wives, children, and parents had all been gassed to death. Men who had been strong and hopeful were now derelicts.

I was not able to visit the Small Lager for several days, but I went early on Sunday morning. Morale had improved considerably, and I noticed that the newcomers had already instituted their own system of barracks justice, not yet as stern as our own, but effective. I saw a Hungarian standing on a table with a sign in large letters hanging from his neck: "I am a despicable thief. I stole my comrade's bread."

We could often tell the state of affairs in the German military machine by little changes in the character or procedure of the transports. This Hungarian group, for instance, was distinguished by the absence of any men between the ages of twenty and twenty-six. They had been taken for labor service to the Eastern Front where German and Hungarian Nazis had slaughtered almost all those who did not manage to cross to the Russian lines. Those who reached Buchenwald were from sixteen to twenty years old, and from twenty-seven up as old as sixty. (The men over fifty had saved themselves from the gas chambers by falsifying their ages.)

Compared to us these men were particularly unfortunate. They were not in Buchenwald to stay. Buchenwald would have been a paradise for them. But they were destined for the "mobile form" of extermination which meant that they would leave on one transport, and another, until they were all dead. Emil went to work and he managed to have about thirty-five of the younger Hungarians assigned to our barracks. We had to crowd up a bit more, but by making it possible for them to remain, we saved the lives of some.

Then we received a serious blow. An order came through that eighty men from the Jewish Block must be chosen for a transport. This was Emil's responsibility. He had to sit down with the list, with himself as counsel and only his own mind to steel him, and select eighty of us for death. If he refused, twice that number would die. Emil did the job. We took leave of many old friends when that transport left the camp. Among them was my friend Precz, but Precz had a charmed life. Of that group of eighty, five were alive and freed on the day of liberation. Only five—but Precz was among them.

There was a frantic insanity about the comings and goings in Buchenwald. The German machine was a little out of control. There was an element of panic in everything the Nazis did. A few days later another huge transport, again of twenty-five hundred men, arrived from Hungary. Again I met many old friends, including men from my section of the country who remembered my mother and spoke kindly of her. Again we did what we could to make the newcomers comfortable.

Nothing in Buchenwald moved me as much as the arrival of those Hungarian transports. They made me think of my mother who raised six children by herself after my father's death in World War I. I thought of my oldest brother who had died in World War I. I thought of my brother Lajos in America who had with such foresight sent for my other brothers and sisters in time to save them from Buchenwald, Ravensbruck, Auschwitz, Marienbad. And I was proud, when I brought food to the new arrivals, that my intimates among them could think of no better way to compliment me than to say, "Jeno, you are your mother's son."

28

In all his years in Buchenwald I doubt whether Emil ever acquitted himself more nobly than when he saved the Russian and Hungarian children. He accomplished a miracle that no inmate of Buchenwald at the time will ever forget.

There were in the camp about fifty Russian children, two of whom, were only ten years old (although officially much older). Since everyone in Buchenwald had to work, these two lived in the Big Lager with the others. They worked in the kitchen.

Morning and evening they stood Appel with the rest of us. Everyone contributed a little to help them dress warmly so that they could survive Winter Appels. During the day they sat around the kitchen, and in the evenings they played with the grown-ups. We all saw to it that they had enough to eat.

It was a triumph on our part that despite Buchenwald, these two children were gay and lively. The other Russian children worked on the night shift, most of them in the shoemaker's shop, so that they did not have to stand Appel.

Then the second large Hungarian transport arrived, and it brought to the camp four hundred and ten children between the ages of thirteen and sixteen! Emil immediately made it his duty to save the lives of these children. First he had to talk to the Nazi officials, and he must have been unusually eloquent because he convinced them that these skinny, starved boys would develop into first-rate workers. Then he arranged to organize four separate children's barracks which would include the Russians and Hungarians.

He ran into difficulties. The "political" fathers immediately saw the sense of this, and understood that their children had a better chance of survival if they supported Emil. Those fathers who were neither "politicals" or organized workers resisted the idea strenuously, and thereby placed the lives of their children in serious danger. Emil finally convinced all except one man who refused to give in—and who left Buchenwald in a death-transport, his son by his side!

Emil arranged for the children to have five weeks of leisure, after which he could stall no longer. Then they were sent out to work. In the evenings the children, most of whom were orphans, visited the various Blocks. One or two of us appointed ourselves foster-fathers for every child. It was our responsibility to get the children extra food, a little clothing, share packages, watch out for their health. Actually we succeeded in establishing what amounted to a family relationship with them. After work each child used to seek out his foster-father in the barracks.

Some of us who were equipped for the task started evening classes for the boys; others gave lectures on subjects which interested them. Our efforts were so successful that the children actually maintained themselves in good physical condition, and had the best possible mental development under the circumstances.

On the day of liberation every child stood in the yard, alive and healthy, clapping for the Allied Armies. This was Buchenwald's greatest miracle.

The children had finally graduated from that macabre school, and today I am sure that whenever they feel grateful for life and the pleasures of living, they think of that stern, unbending, poker-faced man called Emil Korlbach, the man who had never had time to be young.

29

On June 6, 1944, the prisoners of Buchenwald began to believe in life with an intensity and determination that were new in the camp. We sensed the approach of freedom, of all that the word "liberation" meant to us. Castaways on a raft, we saw the rescuing ship in the distance.

The momentous news of the Normandy landings which had breached the "impregnable" West Wall reached us the day they occurred, and unbelievable excitement filled the camp. Men near death revived. The French, particularly, whose home soil was the scene of the landing, were deeply moved. They embraced and kissed one another, Gallic fashion, and constantly lifted their eyes upward as though to look for liberating planes.

Some fellow-prisoners and I rushed to the hospital to visit a young French friend. He was quite overcome by the news, desperately ill as he was, and I was touched when he turned on his side and murmured, "Long live Free France!" I do not know if he said more because we left soon afterward, and he died later that day.

At night we waited for the regular news broadcast with anxious hearts. We were still worried. It was just possible that there was sense to the German boast that they would smash the invaders in the West. But the actions of our captors encouraged us.

Clearly they were astounded, unable to explain, without a policy to meet the situation. Whenever the news announcement became particularly interesting the commandant's thick voice would interrupt over the loudspeaker, shouting, "Es ist befohlen ..." and then he would give some senseless order, shout a prisoner's name, call on someone to report at once, anything at all to drown out the bulletin, his own, his good German news bulletin.

Then we waited for the newspapers, hoping for some details of the landings. Both the Berliner Beobachter and the Thueringer Zeitung honored the invasion by mentioning it, but both avoided any detailed report. We couldn't sleep that night. In the morning we looked into the faces of the SS men. Some of them seemed sulky but there was no indication that they took the landings seriously. Probably their minds had long since ceased to function effectively concerning anything but the miserable routine of their lives in Buchenwald.

One man among us did not surrender to unreasoning excitement. That was Emil. He was sober, cool, exasperatingly every day in manner. He spoke to us in his unemotional voice.

"Don't let yourselves be carried away. Liberation is not much closer than it was the day before yesterday. Remember, we'll be in their hands until the very last minute. Things might be even more serious than they were—not less."

Subsequent issues of the German papers helped us understand the situation in Normandy. We could see that German journalism no longer reflected the unthinking certainty of victory that previously characterized all the papers. The papers did not attribute much importance to the Normandy invasion, but this was a little absurd after months of claiming that the Nazis would beat back an Allied landing.

Writers adopted a tone of pompous calm, stating that forces drawn from the Russian front would easily and in their own time deal with the Allies in the West.

We read how Hitler was relieving one trusted general after another, replacing them with young fanatics. He seemed to sense the approach of the Putsch which would almost cost him his life. He knew that the old Prussian generals would gladly have seen him dead, together with Himmler and his Gestapo. He handed out more honors, more diamond-studded decorations to the younger Nazis, Hitler Jugend members. With these baubles he debauched even more thoroughly the morally diseased youth of Germany. But what was it worth when he had alienated the Prussian generals, the very soul of the Wehrmacht?

After D-Day Buchenwald became busier than ever. The location of the camp was midway between the Red Army on one side, and the British and American armies on the other. Geographically we were as far as possible from liberation.

When the Allied armies were already deep in France, three hundred and eighty Norwegian students arrived in transport. They told us that the Germans were "concentrating" thousands of young Norwegians. For some reason I have not been able to divine, the Norwegians were accorded special treatment. They wore their own clothes without emblems; their heads were not shaved; they used their own bedding; they were not compelled to work; and the Norwegian Red Cross provided their meals, bringing a truck load of the best food for them every day. For the most part they were handsome, athletic young men.

With such privileges, privileges that one might suspect were bribery in Buchenwald, it is still more to their credit that these Norwegians had such a high standard of behavior in regard to other prisoners. They studied among themselves, organized athletics to while away the time. But they exhibited the utmost unselfishness toward others less fortunate. They shared their fine rations with the hungry.

They deprived themselves of meals to feed the children. They stripped themselves of clothing, gave to the threadbare, and then sent home for more clothes. They took the most wretched, the most hopeless, under their protection. And they organized themselves so that they could help in the most systematic way, paying particular attention to those selected for the death transports.

The same was true of the Danish police who were brought to Buchenwald because they had refused to serve the Nazis. They were stripped of their police uniforms, but in other respects they had the same privileged status as the Norwegians, and acted toward us in much the same splendid manner.

Fresh Hungarian transports continued to arrive, but the victims stayed only four or five days before moving on. Out of every transport we managed to smuggle some thirty or forty men into the Big Lager, with Emil's help, and, of course, in secrecy. These, at least, we saved from an imminent death. Our Block became so crowded that a new Block (No. 28) was established, and this, too, rapidly filled up with four hundred men.

A German political prisoner, strict, but just and intelligent, was made the Block Leader.

Summer came on. The American aviators continued to take photographs. One hot July day they visited us twice and we watched in wonder and expectation. Now they did not have to come from England or Italy, but from near-by fields in France.

We correctly interpreted the rush of transports as the beginning of the end. Another aspect of Nazi mentality was revealed. The "mobile form" of extermination moved more slowly. The circle was closing in. But the Nazis still cherished one objective: to keep prisoners and hostages out of Allied hands, and, if necessary, to kill them all rather than turn them over alive.

In one midsummer transport a Hungarian doctor, Bela Neufeld of Nagyszollos, arrived. He had been a widely respected medical figure, one of the staff of the magazine, Korunk. Dr. Neufeld spoke several European languages and was a well-traveled man of broad vision and truly profound scholarship, the best example of what we call the "cultured European." He had been arrested with his seventy-three-year-old father, and since he was a "political," the Nazis had whipped him into unconsciousness in the presence of the old gentleman. Then they turned the tables and beat the father to death in Auschwitz in the presence of the son. But the doctor was physically strong, and he ended in Buchenwald where he could perform useful labor.

We found him rather reserved and it was with difficulty that a few of us established friendly relations with him. Yet the doctor's essential personality broke through his reserve in a little while. He was a man with an instinctive urge to teach those less informed than himself. With little fanfare or even self-consciousness, he began to lecture us on subjects which we found interesting. He had special opportunities to do this at Appel, and he spoke so brilliantly that the ordeal of the count was much easier to bear. He made us feel as though we were no longer in Buchenwald but in some University where the students must stand while the professor addresses them. Although he had never performed manual labor, Dr. Neufeld drew one of the hardest of the construction jobs. He was a man of fifty-three, but he toiled without complaint. In the evenings he would groom himself scrupulously. His zebra-striped suit was always neat, his hands and nails amazingly clean. He was always hungry but he took food from us only after the strongest urging on our part.

Prisoners in leading posts had long planned to provide a daytime teacher for children on the night shift. By this time things were so organized that the children could sleep most of the nights while "on the job." Dr. Neufeld seemed to be the answer to the teacher problem, and Emil actually arranged to have him teach. But it did not last for long.

The Buchenwald command issued an order calling for sixty men from our Block for a transport. Emil had the power of choosing the prisoners, but unfortunately Dr. Neufeld was specifically mentioned in the order by name and number as one who must be included. He was a marked man.

The transport numbered a thousand men, mainly Hungarian Jews from the Small Lager. The report had it that they were to clear away ruins in bombed-out areas. Later we heard that they had gone to Magdeburg which was under constant bombardment. Left among us was a Dr. Moricz Goldman, a sixty-year-old lawyer from Tokay, who had been a close friend of Dr. Neufeld. Although Dr. Goldman had always been one of the more cheerful of us, he fell into a melancholia after Dr. Neufeld's departure.

In the meanwhile two men, both well past sixty, came to our block from the Small Lager. They had been childhood playmates and lifelong friends, and they had shared activities both in the civil and religious communities of their home town of Nyirbator. One was named Nadasi, the other, Barna.

Since they were both vigorous and well the Nazis believed them when they stated their ages as far less than they were. Both men worked hard at their jobs because they knew that at their time of life it was dangerous to be ill or weak in Buchenwald.

Nadasi was eternally hopeful. At his age he still believed passionately in a better future. His smile and optimism became his hallmark. Barna, however, was temperamentally quite different. He could not forget his family, lost in Auschwitz. He always talked of his little grandson, Toni, and would have broken down many times had it not been for Nadasi's cheerful influence. They worked and slept side by side, shared everything they had, and were as inseparable as twins. We never had a moment's trouble with them.

    I was friendly with both of them. Nadasi was known for his inexhaustible supply of Hungarian jokes with which he would regale us during Appel. But poor Nadasi was very near-sighted, and one evening when he was walking back from work, a truck hit him. He was not critically injured but he had to be hospitalized for a head wound. Barna was so disturbed by the accident that that evening after Appel he became ill and also went to the hospital with a high fever. He had pneumonia. Then Nadasi returned and received five days' "indulgence" from work. When the five days ended, he didn't want to return to the job without his friend. He pleaded for another five days' leave, claiming severe head pains, and he got the leave. Then Barna returned and received an eight-day leave. Eventually they returned to work together.

The very day they returned to work SS troopers were going from barracks to barracks to collect convalescents. On their list were the names of Nadasi and Barna. The troopers gathered two thousand men in all, including an entire Block of eight hundred in the Small Lager, composed of men too ill to work.

At this time Auschwitz was near its inglorious close. The Nazis were evacuating and dismantling it to remove every clue to their crimes. Only the gas chambers and the crematorium remained standing in Birkenau, ready for desperate last-minute business. (Those bastards never changed, right to the very end!)

We hoped that Barna and Nadasi would stay with us since they had returned to work. But at the evening Appel Nadasi did not smile and he told no jokes. He stood beside Barna before we went to the yard, and kept telling him there was nothing to fear. After all, they had both been back at work, had they not? We congratulated them on having returned to the job in the nick of time, and we gave them double portions of the jam which had been distributed at supper. Nadasi, however, didn't trust his luck. Before the count began he came to me and entrusted me with some papers, family documents which he asked me to forward if I lived to the day of liberation. I tried to be cheerful.

"Come on, Uncle Nadasi," I said, "they won't take you away."

He didn't answer but simply repeated the request that I keep the papers. Then he said, "You can't pull the wool over my eyes, Jeno, but Barna mustn't suspect anything till the last minute."

He worried only about Barna. Before Appel I stuffed Nadasi's pockets with as much food as possible since no one was allowed to canny packages.

I exchanged my warm overcoat for his lighter one.

Then Barna approached me in the doorway, carrying four large potatoes which some Russians had given him. He asked me to put them in my locker, claiming that they weren't safe in his. He would cook them after Appel. I didn't know what to say to this curious request, so I did as he asked.

We lined up in the yard. It began to rain. Nadasi stood by my side, five men away from Bama. The SS troopers walked along the rows of prisoners, selecting men whose names were on their list. Barna observed the tension. He managed to come over to us, trembling, and ask what was going on.

Nadasi spoke sharply. "Don't be a child, Nicholas. We're sixty-two years old. We have to die sometime."

The SS troopers continued to call names and herd the chosen together at one side of the yard. Each man called had to surrender his one good garment, the overcoat, and throw it on a rapidly growing heap on the ground. The living would need the coats.

In a few minutes Nadasi and Barna were being led away. Barna collapsed halfway across the yard, but Nadasi supported him and they moved on.

Nadasi turned his head and called over his shoulder, "Good-by, my friends! God bless you all!" As they passed the pile of overcoats Nadasi removed first his own, and then gently helped

Barna with his. It was raining more heavily and they stood there, shivering, until the trucks arrived.

They reached Auschwitz the next day where they were among the last group to be exterminated in the gas chambers. Shortly afterward the Nazis tore down the chambers and the crematorium to keep it a great secret from the approaching Red Army.

Two thousand men, of whom four hundred were Jews, made that last trip to Auschwitz. The Germans blamed their deaths on American bombings.

The night Nadasi and Barna left we did little talking in our barracks. By now the majority of our Block was Hungarian and we missed these two men as we had missed few others. Then Emil came in and spoke to us.

"I know you're downhearted," he said in his usual measured fashion. "Learn a lesson from it. Don't let yourselves be carried away by the news, no matter how good it sounds. As long as there is one SS trooper left, the war is still on. There are going to be many mass executions before the end.

Time is short. The fight for survival is only beginning. Don't forget."

We didn't forget.

30

On the night of July twentieth the radio was silent, and this silence, like anything which violated the routine of Buchenwald, was conspicuous. We wondered why we missed our daily dose of propaganda designed either to bolster the prestige of the Nazi regime among us, or to depress us still further. Then whispered rumors spread like grass-fire over the camp. A number of workers returned to the barracks that afternoon with vague reports of a rebellion in Germany.

We didn't dare rejoice. There was too much likelihood that this was rumor, no more. But the reports persisted, and by evening they had the ring of truth. The generals had made an attempt on Hitler's life. Of course, they failed and there was little cause for celebration, but the very attempt was heartening even though Hitler suffered only a superficial wound. Lightning never strikes where the nettles grow, as we used to say.

Appel was late that night. Emil did not appear until half past seven, and I was surprised to find that he was nervous and irritable. Then we went to the courtyard for the count. In summer Appels were usually much shorter since none of us dropped dead from the cold, but this night we were kept waiting for an hour and a half. We did not mind, however, because the weather was fine and we would willingly have spent the entire night there.

We soon discovered the reason for the delay in the Appel. A Polish officer and two Russian soldiers, taking advantage of the confusion following the news of the attempt on Hitler's life, had managed to escape from one of the work gangs during the day, an almost unprecedented feat. Gangs of soldiers went out to search for the fugitives. The loudspeaker announced the escape. SS men ransacked the neighboring territory, beating the forests, scouring the hillsides, but without results.

The count could not begin until the escaped prisoners were found or until the soldiers returned. We could do nothing but wait in the yard. Had this been winter we would have been bitterly angry at these men, but as it was we were glad of the escape and we wished them luck.

At ten o'clock the SS men returned empty-handed. There was no sign of the fugitives. The Buchenwald band was silent that night and for the three following days. Then the band returned, the guards shouted and beat prisoners, men died, and Buchenwald was itself once again.

As always, time went slowly although there was no lack of exciting minutes and hours. We felt confident that the war could not last much longer. With the Russians to the east, and the Americans, British, French, and others to the west, the German machine was bound to crack wide open. Emil, as usual, tried to keep our heads level, to save us from the mistakes of exuberance, and he managed to hold us in check. He felt that the Nazis, whirling in an ever smaller circle, would turn on us with acts of unprecedented desperation. He knew that in every Nazi's mind was the thought, "If I die, you die too." And he never let us forget it although we would gladly have put it out of mind had he given us the chance.

In August a newcomer reached Buchenwald, a man whom I had never met but who was something of a legendary figure to everyone in Germany, friend or foe. The man was Ernst Thaelmann, leader of the German Communist Party, whom the Nazis had held in the dungeon of Moabit for eleven years. When he arrived in Buchenwald the commandant ordered him confined in an individual cell rather than in one of the Blocks.

On August twenty-third some of the men who worked in the crematorium reported that on the previous day the body of Ernst Thaelmann went to the ovens. There was a knife wound in his back and two bullet wounds in his body. A few days later the

Nazis announced that Thaelmann had died in an air raid on August twenty-fourth. But since we had already been told the facts, we knew this to be a lie. We could never ascertain whether the murderer, doubtless some SS man, acted on his own initiative or under orders, but since Thaelmann was in an individual Cell it is practically certain that his murder was official.

31

August 24, 1944, was an oppressively hot day. We worked in our shorts. A friend of mine named Brunner, who had been an Antwerp diamond merchant in civilian life, had received a package from home. It was my custom to cook some things for the men because I had access to a fire in the shop.

Despite the heat, I cooked beans for Brunner. We were planning a feast of bean soup that night. Before I came to Buchenwald my cooking talents extended to coffee and tea, no further, but hunger had taught me a few primitive lessons. Twice the water had boiled away, and twice I had added more to the pot, but the beans refused to get soft. I added a few grains of barley and some garlic, doing all this while I worked. Brunner was outside, pushing a wheel barrow of cement on a construction job.

It was almost noon when the sirens sounded. The American planes were coming again. We felt no inclination to enter the stifling barracks where we were supposed to take refuge when the alarm sounded. I put the pot of beans on one side of the stove to save them from scorching, and set out with my friends in the direction of the woods which surrounded the factory where we intended to lie down in the cool shade until the all-clear sounded. Only one prisoner, the German factory barber, refused to go with us. His barber shop was comfortable enough, and there he could mourn his sons who had "died a heroic death in the service of the Fuehrer and the Fatherland."

As we neared the trees some SS guards rushed after us and drove us back to the barracks. They were following orders. The Nazis knew well enough that the barracks were flimsy and in the event of an air raid would prove the most lethal spot in the camp. The guards themselves, of course, went to the concrete-lined basements.

The SS guards ran wildly about, driving the prisoners out of the woods, but they were only partially successful. Almost fifteen hundred prisoners hid behind trees where they remained since they considered the barracks a death trap.

The prison fire department, with a hundred and twenty men and three modern fire trucks, stood ready in the courtyard.

When we reached our barracks we found that only a few of our Block were absent, but Block 28, the other Jewish Block, was half empty. The missing men were out in the woods. Emil was angrier than I have ever seen him when he heard of this breach of discipline.

In the distance we could hear the planes. The drone came closer and closer, and we knew from the sound that there were many planes. When we could hear the roar quite distinctly Emil suddenly shouted, "Down on the floor! On your stomachs!"

We obeyed. And as we did, I am sure every one of us had the same thought. We had been listening to air-raid warnings day after day, but never did more than enter the barracks, sit around, and ignore the whole business until the all-clear signal. Never had Emil issued a command of this sort during a flight of American planes overhead.

And there he was, shouting, "Down on the floor! On your stomachs!"

Then we knew that no photographers' mission flew overhead. There was not only Emil's command to assure us of this, but also his unusual anger at the men in Block 28 who were in the woods instead of the barracks. We came to the only possible conclusion: Emil and those who worked with him knew something about this American mission which we did not know. And he could not have found it out from the Nazis because had they known it, they would have taken some elementary precautions during the day.

Emil also fell to the floor as soon as he saw that we were obeying him. Then there followed a strange minute or two in which we could hear the beat of our hearts, our neighbor's heavy breathing, and above, the steady hum and drone of the planes. Then a sudden roar, explosions one after the other, the barracks shaking and heaving, the vibrations fluttering through our bodies as though we were struck tuning forks. The noise stopped our ears. The individual explosions lost their identity and merged into a steady roar, sharp whistling, the sound of walls crashing, heavy objects striking the ground, bricks and fragments of stone clattering about the yard, and the whole maelstrom of sound echoing back from the forest.

We were frightened. We knew there was no more exposed spot in Buchenwald than the barracks. Some men jumped to their feet and rushed toward the windows. They would have leaped out to certain death if Emil hadn't sped to intercept them. In the rare seconds of silence he ordered them back, pushed them down, rolled them under tables, and forced them to the floor wherever there was an inch of space.

"Don't move, anyone!" He howled. "Stay here! This is the safest spot in the camp! This is the only place where you've got a chance to live!"

Emil was a man, not a machine, and the excitement of the situation showed in his pale taut face, his unnaturally bright eyes. He moved quickly around the barracks, warning, commanding, demanding, pleading, and begging. We felt trapped, and I myself would have liked to leap for the window and get outside, anyplace beyond those compressing walls, but Emil didn't let a single man leave. Now we could distinguish individual blasts and following each was a deep growling sound as though a town were sinking through the crust of the earth. All our windows were shattered. Part of the roof suddenly collapsed. When it did, our self-discipline snapped. Kurt, Emil's assistant, made a break for the window. A few men followed, and I followed, too, failing for the first time in Buchenwald to obey Emil Korlbach. I know now that I was a little hysterical. I couldn't stick it out there any longer and wait for what I thought was certain burial under the falling roof.

Outside we met the inferno. Buchenwald was a huge unbroken flame; great chunks of masonry flew through the air, ponderous even in flight; smoke blew in crazy patterns. Fire and smoke, shivering buildings and flying debris wherever we turned. The heat was almost unbearable. The very air was on fire and the flames pressed against my face. And the bombs still fell.

Since the hospital was not in the immediate vicinity of the factories we thought it would offer more security. We started to crawl toward it on our bellies. It was not far but the distance seemed endless. More prisoners joined us as we crept along. Apparently all self-restraint had disappeared and the men were rushing from the barracks. A building nearby collapsed with a snapping sound and a strange sigh. A bomb dug into a patch of earth and flung aloft tons of rock and sod. A factory caved inward and from the guts of the building rose a mass of rubbish, dust, and blocks of stone. Cutting through these amorphous noises were the sharp cries and wails of the wounded, all sounding the note of horror, panic, and death-fear. We looked for an exit from the nightmare. Each of us expected his turn in the next second. By degrees we reached the little clump of trees behind the hospital. There we found at least a thousand men, those who had been there since the beginning of the raid, and those who had come since. We felt a little safer. We were under the trees only a few minutes when the bombing suddenly ceased.

There was no sound now accept the crackling of the fires and the occasional collapse of walls. An escort plane circled the camp and dropped leaflets. I picked one up and found that it was an air-newspaper, one of those which then fell over Germany almost every day.

Then more explosions broke the delicate silence. Delayed-action bombs were bursting. The munitions stored in the factories began to go off at intervals of a few minutes, now to our left, now to our right. Smoke blurred our eyes and hid the sun. I could not see well enough to inspect the American newspaper.

Then this last gasp of the raid ended, the slow wind blew the smoke away, the sun came out again. By now we were in an agony of thirst from the smoke and the heat, but we could not move because fires surrounded us on all sides. It was not until two that afternoon that we first received reports of what was happening throughout the camp. Firemen were working desperately to put out the flames. The Weimar Fire Department had come to help. One by one we ventured to rise and look around for our friends in the barracks and elsewhere.

The huge soldiers' barracks and the officers' apartment houses lay in ruins. Of the ten enormous three-story SS barracks, five were leveled, not a stone remained standing. The other five lacked walls, roofs, or both, and they were still smoldering hours later. The beautiful officers' houses with their landscaped gardens were all destroyed. Furniture, some of which we had built, stood outside where the force of the explosion had tossed it. The furniture burned lazily.

The shop where I worked was a huge flambeau since it contained fifty carloads of wood and other inflammable building materials. Our completed or half-completed work crackled merrily. By four o'clock only the great metal machines, twisted and distorted beyond recognition, were left to show that it had been a workshop.

The walls of the large military garage were shattered, and of the few hundred vehicles housed there, not one was worth more than its weight in metal. Two of the three fire trucks were destroyed. The Gustlov Works, largest arms factory in the camp, was now a heap of ashes. Skeletons of machinery, shapeless, tortured pieces of iron, ribs of steel, lay tossed about carelessly. The bath house and the laundry were damaged.

But we looked further at a sight so astounding that it was difficult to believe.

Not one prisoners' barracks had suffered serious damage!

There were eighty-one barracks in the Big Lager. Concussion shattered all their windows, and here and there flying debris damaged a roof, but that was all. In the Small Lager not only the barracks, but even the tents stood as they had before the raid. The camp kitchen was unharmed, the food warehouses intact.

Now we could appreciate those daily photographic missions which flew over Buchenwald. I was a man with too intimate a knowledge of air raids, but never had I seen such accurate bombing.

There were twenty-seven thousand prisoners in camp that day. We picked up five hundred and twenty-one dead prisoners in the woods where they lay after having gone in spite of the Block Leader's advice. One thousand prisoners were wounded, the vast majority of whom had also been outside the barracks.

Almost all the four thousand SS men in camp were in secure shelters during the raid. Yet of these, seven hundred died and many more were wounded. The SS officer who was assistant to the commandant lost his wife and three children.

Many of the tenants of Block 28, the Hungarian-Jewish Barracks, were killed in the woods, mostly from the effect of fire-bombs. My friends Czukor and Sapir were luckily unharmed.

Twenty-four American planes carried out the mission. It lasted only eleven minutes.

There were other reasons for the amazing performance of these planes. The cream of our Buchenwald Underground, the most trustworthy and tested anti-fascists, were in constant contact with Allied aviators. There was actually secret radio communication between our Underground and the Allied forces. The Underground furnished information which photographs could not reveal. I had been more or less in the confidence of leading members of the Underground, including Emil, and they had given me hints of this although they always stopped short of revealing their plans or the details of their work.

During the raid Emil could not explain to us why we were safe in the barracks. He could not reveal that only a half hour before he had been communicating with the Americans, and that the commander of the bombing squadron had himself ordered prisoners to remain in the barracks. But by disobeying Emil, five hundred and twenty-one men lost their lives and more than a thousand suffered wounds. Emil could not explain because had there been one traitor there, only one, the Nazis would have machine-gunned the lot of us as soon as the raid ended. Again he had made a terrible choice and allowed hundreds to go to their deaths to save the lives of thousands.

Kurt, Emil's subordinate, second in rank and prestige only to Emil—even Kurt did not know these details at the time. Only Emil and his immediate associates knew, and they had long since learned to keep their counsel.

The air newspaper I retrieved during the raid was written in German and featured an appeal by General Paulus, who had been taken prisoner at Stalingrad. The General claimed that the war was over and the Germans should surrender to save futile bloodshed. The loss of any more lives would be a wanton waste. Hitler was prolonging the war for one reason: to postpone, if even for a day, his death and the death of his clique. The Fuehrer was ready to sacrifice countless young Germans for that end.

But we were in Buchenwald where the SS murder detachments knew that to be taken prisoner would mean the gallows. Yet during and after the raid we were treated to a rare spectacle. Now, for the first time, we could observe the deportment of the Hitler heroes, the great SS men, the troopers and the officers, not when they faced half-starved and helpless men, but when they came up against an enemy more powerfully armed than themselves. We examined the conduct of hangmen when it was their turn to march to the scaffold.

Their faces changed. They were no longer the frozen or twisted masks of ersatz heroes. They were the faces of frightened men, sick with fear.

After the bombing ended the raging fires prevented us from paying any attention to the wounded for two hours. The commandant shouted hysterical orders over the one remaining loudspeaker.

"Every doctor, nurse, and medical worker! Report at once in the Appel yard!"

"All prisoners report at once to collect the wounded!"

For hours the loudspeaker blared forth commands. The commandant frantically sought to gather together everyone who had the least bit of training in hospital work. He forgot to ask whether physicians were Jewish or Mohammedan. Doctors who had been working on construction gangs, surgeons whose hands had become gnarled and calloused, rushed to the hospital. Jewish physicians went without question to fulfill the obligations of their profession and save lives. From our own Block Dr. Frieder of The Hague, and a young Transylvanian named Dr. Rosenberg, did outstanding work, operating with pocket knives for hours on end.

Belgian and French physicians performed operations with their hardened swollen hands, and the moral superiority of the human being over the Hitler German was apparent in that these prisoners were as conscientious with SS patients as with fellow-inmates. More than one doctor was wounded himself, but men worked on despite their wounds, sweat pouring from their faces in the hastily improvised operating tents.

We who were unharmed removed the dead and wounded from the ruins. We took the living to a roofless first aid station, and the dead to the crematorium. Ironically enough, that ghastly structure had escaped damage. A bomb which fell in the crematorium courtyard turned out to be a dud. As it happened, this was fortunate since hundreds of corpses lay in the camp amid odd hands, torn-off limbs, headless torsos, bodiless heads, and the carnage gave off a horrible odor in the summer evening heat. For once the crematorium served a needed purpose.

The two hospitals, one for prisoners and one for soldiers, were not sufficient to house the injured. The Nazis, of course, not being capable of conduct equal to that of our doctors, saw to it that SS men were treated first, and then the prisoners.

The assistant commandant rushed about like a madman, tearing his hair and moaning. He, whose wife and three small children had been killed, was suddenly learning to appreciate what such a tragedy means. The SS soldiers beneath the ruins, many still alive but with arms or feet pinned by tons of stone, lay bleeding, dying—singing different tunes from their usual ones. History will record that there was little of the Siegfried in their conduct. They whimpered; they whined. They faced death like the amoral cowards that they were—pigs stuck in a fence and squealing. Yesterday they had stood at our backs with whips, and kicked us with their polished boots. Now they murmured, "Kamerad, help me! Get this girder off! God bless you!"

Wasn't it amazing? Suddenly we Jews, with our Star of David emblem and our shaven heads and our gassed families in Auschwitz—suddenly we Jews were "Kamerad!"

But they miscalculated. Coming from their lips, the term failed miserably to endear them to us.

Luckily we were able to rescue the prisoners more easily than the Nazis, since the prisoners were mainly in the open woods while the SS, who had been under cover, had to be dug out from the rubble. It took two days to gather up all the victims of the raid, and during those two days we lived off the fat of Buchenwald. Never before did we receive such fine food, such considerate treatment. They gave us meat, not once, but twice a day, to induce us to speed the rescue work. Speed was essential if we were to save many trapped in the suffocating basements beneath the wrecked buildings. Only the prisoners were available for this work, and our lives were suddenly precious to the Nazis.

Strangest of all, the very gates of Buchenwald were left unlocked and unguarded. We could have walked out at will. Yet not one of us left the camp.

It was logical enough. Our uniforms, our hairdress, branded us. Germany itself was now nothing but a huge prison. To walk out was to walk to death. The circle had closed tighter and tighter and wherever we went we would find ourselves in a cage surrounded by the fear-maddened hyenas of Hitlerism. Bombs fell everywhere. Berlin, Cologne, Frankfurt, Düsseldorf—all in ruins, and the inhabitants living in terror. There was no food. Everyone in Germany was hungry. There could be no escape from Buchenwald other than liberation.

For two days we were spared Appel, and when it resumed on the third day, no band played marches. The band was again in mourning, and again the mourning lasted three days.

In Block 22 only nine men were missing, but Block 28 suffered twenty-three dead and seventy wounded, all recently arrived Hungarians. When I returned to the Block many of my friends, who supposed me dead, were overjoyed to see me.

Slowly life returned to the Buchenwald routine.

We speculated on a few problems. What would become of us prisoners if there was no work to do, no factories or shops, no buildings to build? It would take live years to repair the damage of that air raid, and there seemed little likelihood that the Germans would attempt it. They had no guarantee that American planes wouldn't return when the work was started, and reduce the place to ruins once again. But if they did not restore the buildings, would they simply keep us there, feed us and house us?

There were few camps left to which we might be transferred. Emil's constant cautioning took on a new and more terrible meaning. The logic of Buchenwald was marking us all for death! We could not imagine our captors turning us over to the Allies to bear witness against them. Having murdered millions, why should they not murder a few thousand more?

The radio began to function again three days after the raid. On August thirty-first the news broadcasts resumed and the commentator reported the bombing of Buchenwald:

"The American terror-bombers, on the twenty-fourth of this month, bombed the camp at Buchenwald. Five hundred and fifty prisoners were killed, and fourteen hundred seriously injured. Among the dead was Ernst Thaelmann, the leader of the German Communists."

The communique did not mention the tremendous toll of German dead and wounded or that Thaelmann had been cremated two days earlier.

The next day another communique described how German anti-aircraft had brought down four of the American bombers, a ridiculous fabrication since no anti-aircraft was in operation during the raid.

Soon after the raid I wandered back to the shop, or rather to what was left of it. Although there were ruins all around, I found my pot of beans still standing on the stove, but for all my precautions, they were scorched!

When we were finally ordered to report to our regular labor gangs, they put us to work clearing away ruins. In a few days we began rebuilding the soldiers' barracks and the officers' homes. They evidently did not intend to rebuild the factories but they planned to salvage my shop since they needed its products for the barracks construction. We stayed and worked as carpenters. Lumber arrived piece-meal, and according to plans the shop was to be in operation by December, New machines arrived, this time from dismantled and evacuated concentration camps in the path of the Allied Armies.

The status of Jewish stone-masons suddenly rose to a new high since there was great need of them to provide shelter for the men and officers of the SS and their families. Their families were with them because they had believed Buchenwald to be safe from air raids.

The stone-masons were given extra rations of bread and soup, and all of us received another unprecedented consideration—a ration of fifteen or twenty cigarettes each week.

We went ahead with the work gladly because we thought the liberating armies would have need of the barracks and apartments. We felt as though we were building for them rather than for the Nazis.

The atmosphere of German arrogance was now considerably modified. The bombs had shattered more than the buildings of Buchenwald. They had smashed the idiotic yet persistent dream of invincibility.

32

As the weeks passed the SS men, aided by short memories, regained some of their assurance, and with it their usual brutality.

In the months past I had become friendly with a young Frenchman named Jean who worked with me in the shop. He became ill and was taken to the hospital. One night I went alone to visit him there, and I was shocked to find him in an obviously moribund state. I do not know what disease brought him there, but in our general condition any disease could easily prove fatal.

Jean talked little to me and the few words he spoke obviously cost him precious energy. Finally he motioned me to lean over and he whispered a request. "Jeno," he said, "will you get me a priest?"

I had a moment's conflict during which I wondered whether to pretend to him that he was not dying, but I looked at his face and saw that pretense was useless. I said, "All right, Jean," and then I left the hospital for the French barracks.

Although Buchenwald regulations forbade any religious ceremonies or manifestations, I decided to chance it so that Jean would get whatever comfort was possible in his last moments. I knew that there was a young priest in the French barracks, and I soon found him, dressed in the standard prisoner garb, with the shaved head, emblems, and number. Briefly I told him the situation and he followed me out to the hospital.

The priest knew very well the risk he was taking, but he was a simple and honest man to whom religion meant a way of life and a duty to others. I walked with him to Jean's bedside and then stood back, partly to make myself unobtrusive, and partly to try to block the view from the attendant on guard. But as the priest began the death-bed ceremony of his church, his actions became obvious and the hospital attendant ran down the corridor to the bedside.

He seized the priest by the shoulder, swung him around, and kicked him viciously in the groin. In a paroxysm of pain, the priest tried to turn back to the bed and continue the devotions, but the hospital attendant seized him again, kicked him brutally, and pushed him toward the door, beating him as he went. Jean looked helplessly from his bed, bewilderment in his eyes, as though he were unable to understand this last and final indignity. He died shortly after, without the consolation of his faith.

When September came, about fifty men in my own Block, men who were deeply religious, came to me, whom they knew to be friendly with Emil, to ask if I would intercede with him and gain them permission to hold a Yom Kippur service. Yom Kippur is the Day of Atonement, the holiest day of the Jewish faith. The fifty who sought permission were mostly newcomers, since Buchenwald life had long since driven such thoughts from the minds of the more religious old-timers. I approached Emil with their request.

Emil had the authority to excuse people from work for a day or two and give them permission to remain in the barracks, but he told me that he could not chance it with fifty men. He might manage it for twenty-five or so, but the absence of fifty men would be much too obvious.

I brought this message to the group, and they choose from among themselves the twenty-five who would remain in the barracks for the ceremony. When Appel ended that night the sun was already down. Yom Kippur is a fast day which begins at sundown, and therefore the celebrants did not want to eat. Emil argued with them. He told them that in Buchenwald they would never survive a fast the following day unless they ate the evening meal. Then he brought them twenty-five pieces of bread and gave instructions that the men must eat it. They did as he said.

When they finished the bread, we posted guards at the windows to keep a watch for intruders. Emil turned to the twenty-five and said, briefly, "Pray low."

The barracks fell silent. Soon the quiet chant of the Kol Nidre, the ritual prayer for the dead, rose in whispered voices through the barracks, and all of us returned in memory to our childhood days and the days of our dim free past.

33

Love in Buchenwald was as systematic and organized as every other phase of our life. The Buchenwald brothel will always remain, together with the Buchenwald band, as one of the true symbols of German fascism.

The brothel was established for the use of all "Aryan" prisoners. Jews were not permitted to patronize the "Aryan" prostitutes. The twenty-five or thirty women who worked in the brothel were all formerly inmates of concentration camps, and whether they were previously prostitutes is highly doubtful although the Nazis spread the rumor that they had volunteered for the present duties! The brothel was a private venture and the women were nominally independent.

Yet it was not a thriving enterprise, partly because there was so much red tape connected with a Buchenwald assignation, and partly because at least eighty per cent of the prisoners were entirely indifferent to sexual matters after a few months in Buchenwald.

The SS soldiers, having facilities of their own, were also denied the use of the brothel. All the Russian soldiers boycotted the institution since they regarded dealings with prostitutes as mutually debasing. There remained the "Aryan" prisoners, principally the Block Leaders, the camp aristocracy.

The one visit per month permitted "Aryan" prisoners was no easy affair. It was preceded by a typically long-drawn out rigmarole. First the man had to present his application to the Block Leader who passed it on to the man in charge of the brothel, and he, in turn, forwarded it to the petitioner's Block Fuehrer who was always an SS man.

The Block Fuehrer then investigated the man closely to make sure he was not Jewish. Having passed this test, the applicant then underwent a physical examination, and if he got a clean bill of health, he then paid two marks.

The two marks bought a written permit.

But this was only the first stage. Then the man had to wait. There was no way to determine how long the period of waiting might last. Often it was two months and the applicant discovered that a prior appointment with the crematorium intervened, and the anticipation of love was consumed with his body in the busy ovens. If, however, he was more fortunate, he would stand at Appel one evening with his myriad fellow-prisoners, and suddenly hear the loudspeaker bawl out his name and number, announcing to the entire camp that he was to present himself at the brothel the following day.

Since the women in the brothel entertained only in the day time, an appointment meant excuse from work. This, in itself, might have impelled some men to apply for permits. Just as a man was permitted six minutes in the Auschwitz gas chambers, he was permitted ten minutes—no more, no less—in the brothel.

The record does not state what became of the two marks, but it is not likely that the prostitutes received it all. Surely some of it went to the commandant, the camp treasury, or the

German war fund. Most likely it went to the camp treasury as payment for the women's board and rent. The authorities never overlooked such niceties of financial arrangements, and their thoroughness in such matters was absolute.

After the war ended Dr. Bela Neufeld, who left the camp to work in a bombed-out area, wrote me a letter in which he discussed the failure of the prisoners to patronize the brothel. "The sexual side of concentration camp life," wrote the doctor, "exhibited characteristics that are worthy of attention.

Sex life, perforce, ceased from lack of opportunities for its satisfaction. But more interesting and fundamental still is the fact that sexual desire did not make its appearance during the period of imprisonment.

This was the general experience, as attested to unanimously by the prisoners themselves. In our normal lives sex plays an important part. Here in the camp, where the instinct of self-preservation dominated, sex withdrew to the background. What will I eat? This was the basic anxiety, and every effort was directed toward securing sufficient nourishment.

Clearly the vital question of maintaining life was so all-embracing that the sex urge did not make itself felt. When bread and sex compete with each other, sex becomes Secondary. Primum vivere.

"Our experiences in the camp for men may be supplemented by the information gathered from the women's camps: one hundred per cent of the female prisoners ceased to menstruate at the very beginning of their term of captivity; the function did not reappear until months after their liberation. This phenomenon was obviously not caused by the change of diet (the lack of vitamins and proteins in the camp rations), but primarily by emotional causes—by shock. This conclusion may be drawn from the fact that the menstrual process ceased suddenly and simultaneously on a mass scale, and with it the libido also became passive. There can be no doubt that sex dominates only under normal conditions. In circumstances where life itself is threatened, the urge for self-preservation becomes the primary impulse."

Dr. Neufeld himself returned to Buchenwald that same September, following the great August air raid. When he arrived he was in a piteous state, all bones in a bag of skin, his wasted body covered with suppurating sores. He sent me a note from the Small Lager to inform me of his arrival, and I hurried over with his friend, Dr. Goldman. We found him among eight hundred men crammed together, the living, the dead, and the dying.

Although we had permits the attendants were reluctant to admit us. We shouted Dr. Neufeld's name and at last caught sight of him, seated on a stool at the far end of the barracks. He gulped the food we had brought with animal voracity. We had difficulty believing it was the same Dr. Neufeld who had left us two months before. He had grown a full beard, not through choice, and this man who was almost fanatical regarding personal cleanliness, was filthy and odoriferous. Since there was no crematorium in Magdeburg where he had labored, they had sent him back to Buchenwald to die.

The next day we collected all the food we could lay our hands on and took it to the starving men, but most of them were beyond help. We managed to take eighteen of them, including Dr. Neufeld, into the Big Lager, thereby saving their lives.

But fortunately Dr. Neufeld had managed to retain his greatest asset: a calm, clear and scholarly mind that survived Buchenwald and Magdeburg.

34

Buchenwald officials never forgot the Polish officer and the two Russian soldiers who escaped the day of the attempted Putsch against Hitler. The German radio broadcast descriptions of the prisoners; posters with photographs of the men hung in every town and city; but there were no results.

One evening in October we stood in the yard for the count, watching the weird shadows our bodies made in the floodlights, while the band played and a touch of frost in the weather aroused in us a dread of the coming winter and the horrors of future Appels.

The yard was the same as always except for a low platform in the center. We looked at it with apprehension because there could be no mistaking its purpose. I had seen its like many times in photographs, movies, and in reality, too, since the day Hitler first set out to master the world. It was a gallows.

We looked at one another.

"What's that doing here?"

Someone put our common suspicion into words.

"There's going to be a public hanging."

Never before in Buchenwald had a man been executed in the sight of other prisoners, save for those whose deaths we witnessed from the windows of the shop. The SS men usually did their butchering in the basement below the crematorium, in the Experimental Block, the hospital, or the yard where the officers kept their horses. I do not know why they chose to be so private about so public a policy of extermination.

The rough gallows was an arch-like arrangement of three wooden beams with long hooks dangling from the crossbeam at the top. The sight of death was certainly no novelty to the twenty-five or thirty thousand men in the camp, every one of whom had observed death daily, often hourly, in Buchenwald.

Yet cold sweat broke out at the prospect of having to witness a planned, cold-blooded, and passionless murder. We wondered who would be the victim of this edifying spectacle.

The SS concluded the count quickly that evening because they wanted to get to the more important business at hand. When it ended we hoped we would be permitted to return to the barracks so that we should not have to witness the hanging, but such hope was absurd. We were to be taught a lesson, and we could not leave the schoolroom.

As soon as the count ended a hollow voice rang out over the loudspeaker:

"Peter Krivicsky, Polish prisoner who escaped from the camp with two companions on July twentieth, has been found, and has been sentenced by the camp commandant to die by the rope as punishment for his act." To that announcement was added the inevitable detail of the man's number since in the account books of fascism the number is all-important.

According to the terms of the Geneva Convention a prisoner-of-war or internee who escapes from confinement may be punished by a maximum of fourteen days in prison. Such was the practice in civilized armies where neither enemy soldiers nor civilians could be given a more severe sentence. German prisoners who escaped in Canada, for instance, or England, served their two weeks and then returned to their regular prisoner-of-war status. The Hitler gang had also signed the Geneva Convention, and now they were honoring it—with the rope.

We had heard rumors that the escaped Polish officer had been captured in Warsaw, and though we fully expected the SS men to kill him, we did not dream it would be a public exhibition. The vindictiveness of the SS was boundless. The hanging was to erase the humiliation of the escape, because escape represented the outwitting of the master-race by an inferior breed.

Nazi justice moved rapidly in that courtyard. Hardly had the announcer's voice faded out when we saw the Polish prisoner walk toward the gallows, an SS soldier at either side of him. The victim wore the regulation zebra-striped uniform, and wooden shoes. His hands were bound behind him. He was calm, manly, dignified. When the group reached the gallows the SS men made the Pole stand on a three-legged stool beneath the noose. At that moment the official executioner walked up to the condemned man.

At that moment the Pole cried out, in a voice harsh but steady, speaking in his native language, "You may murder us by the millions, but we will win. It will be our turn yet!" The noose around his neck cut off whatever else he might have had to say. The executioner kicked the stool from under his feet. The man dropped. His face contorted and turned blue in the cold floodlights, his staring eyes bulging from his head. He kicked once or twice and then stopped moving. The cold October wind swung his body back and forth until it swayed like a pendulum ticking off the last minutes of German fascism.

The commandant did not dismiss us. He let us remain there for a long time to watch our murdered comrade. The example must sink in!

An hour later two prisoners removed the officer's body and laid it on the ground. They handled it as though it were a thing of great delicacy and value — and so it was. Two others placed the body on a stretcher and carried it toward the crematorium.

The commandant who passed sentence on that' Polish officer is today (at the end of 1946) in the hands of American authorities in Germany, but I have heard neither of his trial nor his execution. Is there no rope available?

35

October, 1944, began the nightmare within the nightmare—a terrible winter during which the SS committed at least forty thousand murders in Buchenwald. This figure is so gigantic that it is almost meaningless, but every murder involved a man, an anti-fascist, who bled and suffered agonies in one of the weirdest bursts of mass sadism in the world's entire history.

Other concentration camps in the path of Allied armies were closed or dismantled, or fell before conquering troops. In each case the Nazis herded the prisoners out. Transport followed transport. There was no place to put prisoners, no food to give them, no medicine, no doctors, and no work. There could be only one solution to this problem from the Nazi point of view. That solution was death.

We could hardly keep count of the transports and evacuations. In November nine hundred men of a Hungarian group which had set out, five thousand strong, from Yugoslavia, arrived in Buchenwald.

They had been in "labor service" on the Eastern Front, under the command of Hungarian Nazis. Hungarian Nazi youth received machine guns from the Germans, and they tested the guns on the labor service men. The guns worked.

Then the march back began. Hungarian Nazis escorted the prisoners as far as Austria, by which time a thousand men died. The march took two months, and the prisoners were not allowed to fall out of line to perform natural functions. They arrived in Austria covered with filth and excrement. German Nazis then took over, and they were actually less brutal than their Hungarian imitators. The Germans, at least, let the prisoners bathe before continuing the march.

The nine hundred who reached Buchenwald alive found thousands of Christian Hungarians, active in the Resistance, already in the camp. During the ordeal of admission forty of the group dropped dead under the showers. Among those left living I found a Dr. Nicholas Szekely who had been a childhood friend of my brother Lajos. He was the man who told me the entire story.

The new prisoners were housed in the Small Lager where all sanitary precautions had broken down and an epidemic of dysentery raged. There was no medicine or doctors and it is doubtful whether either would have been of any use. Dr. Szekely himself died three weeks after his arrival.

At the end of December only four of the nine hundred Hungarians were alive.

More new ones came, and still more. The barriers between Jew and non-Jew disappeared in the Small Lager into which Frenchmen, Belgians, Serbs, Hollanders, Poles, Russians, Czechs, Hungarians were crowded. Conditions grew increasingly chaotic. The Nazis threw up a new barracks in the Small Lager, taking men from the Big Lager to act as attendants and Block Leaders. These new appointees began to replace the Ukrainian White Guard prisoner-officials who up until then had run things their own way.

Our new prisoner-leaders managed to see that many of these fascist elements were selected for transports leaving the camp, where they met a fate they richly deserved. When they had been in control, four to five hundred men had died each week in the Small Lager. The sick lay untended on the floor and Ukrainian or Polish White Guardists often deliberately trampled the ailing men to death by jumping on their throats in heavy military boots, cracking their windpipes.

The "mobile form" and the stationary form" of execution now merged into a new standard method. Since the transports which left Buchenwald had no place to go, the SS guards finished off the prisoners somewhere along the road, and then returned for more.

As the number of prisoners in the camp increased, the food decreased proportionately. Our individual rations dwindled to a few crumbs. There was plenty of food in the warehouses but now the Nazis were husbanding these stores because the food situation throughout Germany was desperate. Starvation, too, served as a weapon of murder, and the Nazis used it to the full before the liberating armies arrived.

December, January, and February passed in the same fashion but the tempo of the torture increased. More tension, less bread, a growing feeling of uncertainty. Death had never before been so omnipresent in this vast graveyard of Buchenwald. The Nazis were planning the evacuation of all concentration camps, but they attempted to accomplish this by transporting prisoners from one place to another, and killing them en route. They blew up their abandoned prisons or burned them hoping to leave not even one mute stone to testify to what had happened within the gates.

In January we again learned the value of Emil's wisdom. We were desperate, yes, but we were also positive that victory was close. Toward the end of January a number of Marxists among the prisoners, anxious to express their defiance of fascism and their belief in their coming liberation, talked about holding a secret celebration of Lenin Memorial Day.

Emil, who certainly would have wanted to commemorate the memory of Lenin, would have nothing to do with the proposed celebration, which he considered adventurism, no matter what the motives of the men. Yet eighteen prisoners, including a Block Leader, made plans for the celebration in one of the barracks. They found a young man who played the violin in the camp orchestra who agreed to play for them. They held the celebration one night late in January. The young man played the "Internationale" on a muted violin."

But when the violinist returned to his own Block, an SS guard intercepted him and demanded to know where he had been with his instrument. I do not know the details of what happened after that, but the eighteen men disappeared and we never saw them again. They were heroic men, but in the proximity of liberation they abandoned the discipline that meant so much to every anti-fascist in the camp and was essentially more anti-fascist in character than the determination to flaunt a political celebration in the face of an enemy who still had twenty times our strength.

In the month of March Buchenwald became the last and final stop for all imprisoned anti-fascist Europe. The ring was contracting around Weimar. The Germans claimed that the Americans were sixty-five kilometers away, but the prisoners' grapevine put the figure at twenty-five kilometers.

When Buchenwald became the last camp, it also became a death camp in the official sense, in the sense of Auschwitz and Birkenau. The Germans planned to destroy Buchenwald. That could mean only that they planned to destroy the prisoners as well.

Every new prisoner who arrived strengthened the logic of this unhappy theory. Only American and British war prisoners could hope for life since they were under the jurisdiction of the regular German Army rather than the SS murderers. There were still regular German Army men who were genuinely surprised to discover that the stories of SS brutalities were actually true.

The Nazi Gauleiters, the SS commandants and men, watched their territory shrink to a festered spot on the face of Europe, but they made it all too clear to us that they would show no mercy while they still had arms in their possession. At the end of March we had reached our greatest population—forty-three thousand men—and the SS officers who appeared before us barked orders with the same confident voices they had used in 1942, before the debacle of Stalingrad. The crematorium poured out its smoke unabated.

By March twenty-ninth no one was allowed to leave the camp for outside work or any other purpose. We received bread only four times a week, and if a fugitive piece of meat had ever floated in the thin soup, no such miracle occurred then. The SS had a sty filled with a swarm of pigs and suckling's, and a good herd of cattle. These they displayed to the Red Cross, claiming that they were raised for the prisoners' consumption. The thin slice of salami, supposedly weighing 25 grams, which we had formerly received once a week, now disappeared from the fare. Germany's transportation system was smashed, and there was no way to bring food to the camp even if the wish existed.

The Norwegians and Danes, whose countries had been liberated, left the camp. Packages which had formerly helped us alleviate our constant hunger, stopped coming. The Swiss Red Cross sent packages, but the Nazis confiscated them and diverted the contents to their own tables. We were all starved, all hovering dimly between life and death.

I saw a man eating grass in the little wood, his head hanging apathetically, his eyes filmed over. He asked me a question. "A thousand-pound ox lives on grass and hay," he said querulously. "Why can't an eighty-pound man do it?" I didn't know the answer. I, too, weighed eighty pounds at the time.

36

We did not work on April first, which was Easter Sunday, nor the Monday following, but on Tuesday we reported to the shop as usual. At three o'clock that afternoon the guards dismissed us. We could hear American artillery roaring in the distance. The radio had apparently stopped functioning for all time, and we prisoners were now quite used to the sound of Allied guns.

We were preparing to report for Appel on April third when it was unaccountably canceled. We felt a peculiar strain. No work, no Appel. What good could come of this strange procedure, this ominous idleness? We were anxious and in our anxiety we even forgot our hunger. We would actually have welcomed the call to Appel.

At six o'clock that evening Herman Pister, the commandant, ordered the two chief prisoner-officials to his office. Originally there had been three chief prisoner-officials but one of these had been implicated in that unfortunate Lenin Memorial celebration where "forbidden songs were played by a prisoner-violinist."

The prisoner-officials later reported to us what transpired during that interview. They knocked on the commandant's door and entered. Colonel Pister looked up and said, "I've been ordered to evacuate Buchenwald. I'm not going to carry out the order. I have no more communication with Berlin. I propose to turn over the camp to the Americans as it stands. In return for this, I ask for your assurance that no harm will come to my family."

Since he had asked guarantees only for his wife and children, the prisoners readily agreed to the proposal. They promised to use all their influence with American officials to protect the commandant's family.

The commandant's request was an interesting commentary on his mind. He fully expected the Americans to treat his wife and children as he would have dealt with the dependents of a conquered foe. According to his philosophy the family would suffer for the misdeeds of its lord, Herman Pister. He knew that to ask for protection for himself was an absurdity.

Evidently the Russians were in Berlin, which accounted for the broken communications. An hour after the interview came the official announcement that there would be no "evacuation," which the prisoners interpreted to mean there would be no mass slaughter. We were all dazed with joy. Each one of us felt as though he were already a free man. And to seal his last-minute bargain, Colonel Pister ordered meat, bread, and butter for our supper! Another day or two and then—liberation! We hugged one another in our excitement, and each man welcomed his friend as though he had returned from the dead.

But beyond the camp the American detachments, which were actually only twenty-five kilometers away, suddenly came to a halt and straightened their lines. The Germans organized a last-gasp counter-attack on one flank, and this, too, delayed American arms. On April fourth we were still confident that we would not die, but the silence of the American guns disturbed us.

In the turrets of Buchenwald the armed guards stood as always, their control of us undiminished. The kitchen served bread and soup at noon instead of in the evening, but the food had already lost the good taste it had had yesterday. Doubts crept back into our minds. We recalled other broken promises, remembered the intrinsic worthlessness of a Nazi pledge. But we continued to hope.

Our faces drawn, we stood about in little clusters, consoling each other with our theories. There was no more work. Only the tailor shop, the shoe shop, and the locksmith shop were operating, and even there little actual work was accomplished. The SS soldiers themselves were growing more excitable by the minute, and therefore more dangerous, as they rushed about in a witless manner, waiting for orders to abandon camp.

Then lightning struck from the clear sky.

The loudspeaker, suddenly revived, clamored with orders.

"One hour from now every Jew must report to the Appel yard. Block Leaders will see to it that

Jews mingling with Aryans in the Aryan Blocks are separated and appear promptly in the Appel yard."

It was five o'clock. We looked at one another aghast. The loudspeaker added a further order. "Jews in the hospital are not exempt. The same applies to Jewish doctors assigned to Aryan Blocks."

No "evacuation!" I cursed myself bitterly for having been so stupid as to believe that, if only for one day. A verbal compact with a Nazi commandant! And we were fools enough to place a speck of faith in it!

What could have occurred to make this frightened mass-murderer, Colonel Pister, change his tactics so abruptly? It couldn't have been orders from Berlin. From Weimar, then? Was the Gauleiter sulking and demanding action from his Buchenwald colonel?

But these speculations were barren before the clear fact. There was going to be an "evacuation," and it would begin with the Jews, and then proceed, perhaps by nationalities, perhaps by Blocks. And what a farce was this talk of "evacuation" when there was no place to go other than the grave!

The two Jewish Blocks now numbered about eight hundred and fifty men, while there were two thousand five hundred Jews in the Small Lager, scattered among the "Aryans." Apparently the Nazis planned to take us to the highway and machine-gun us there, deriving what pleasure they could from watching the dashing of our premature hopes.

Immediately we all turned to Emil for advice, for salvation and leadership. We knew that Emil would not lose his head, just as he had not lost it when he had been sentenced to death and led to the place of execution in the early days of his imprisonment. It was no novelty for him to wait for death.

Emil gathered us together in the Block to say a few words. He spoke calmly, as though he were calling us for Appel, but his words were new words, and the character of what he said was completely different from any advice he had ever given us.

"Listen closely. Stay inside the Block. Don't go to the Appel yard. Stay right where you are until I come back. If the guards order you out, say you can't go without your Block Leader." He paused a moment to let this sink in, and then said, "Dismissed."

In the other Jewish Block the leader was an "Aryan," but he gave the men there exactly the same instructions. They were to remain in the barracks and disobey all counter orders.

Emil and the other Block Leader then went to consult with the chief prisoner-officials who had made the pact with the commandant. When he was gone we watched the Appel yard fearfully. Guards were bringing out from the Small Lager those Jews whom they were able to identify among all the mixed nationalities and religions there. The Lager police, themselves prisoners, went into every barracks and ordered the Jews to step forward. Those who were afraid, or who dared not deny that they were Jewish, obeyed. Some fifteen hundred Jews finally stood in the Appel yard.

Six o'clock came and went. Silence, even in the yard, save for the shuffling of feet. At six-thirty the loudspeaker bawled out:

"Where are the Jews? We ordered all Jews to report to the Appel yard! March out at once, every one of you!"

No one obeyed. The fifteen hundred in the yard waited but no more joined them. The Lager police came to our barracks, looked around, and commanded us to go out. Kurt spoke for us. "We can't go without the Block Leader," he said.

The police left without a word, and a few minutes later fully armed SS troopers burst in. "Get a move on in here! Out in the yard!"

Kurt repeated the excuse.

Then something strange happened. The SS men accepted the excuse without insisting, or threatening, or pushing us around. They departed in silence.

By half past seven Emil and his colleagues had not yet returned. The Jews who were standing in the yard finally drifted over to our barracks. At eight o'clock the Appel was canceled. And finally

Emil came back. The Jews from the Small Lager left us to go to their own places.

Emil was gloomy when he entered the barracks. We sat down to listen to his report.

On Tuesday the commandant had evidently believed the Americans would arrive the next day, and since he had received no orders from Berlin he had made his bargain with the prisoner-leaders. Well and good, but the Americans had not arrived on Wednesday, nor Thursday. Orders came through from the regional Gauleiter in Weimar that Colonel Pister must begin evacuating the camp at once. According to Emil the Colonel claimed to have replied, "It's not possible. I haven't got enough soldiers to evacuate forty-three thousand men."

Then the Gauleiter had suggested he do it by groups. "First the Jews, then . . ."

The commandant reflected on this suggestion. Perhaps he could eat his cake and have it, too. Evacuating only the Jews did not constitute, in his eyes, a serious breach of contract, and surely the "Aryan" prisoners would not reproach him on this account. Emil and the others had held him off this night. But what of the next and the next?

Groups of us gathered to discuss it among ourselves, and the men with whom I talked agreed not to spend the night in the Jewish Block. The struggle to stay alive was now an open, acknowledged struggle, just as the decision to murder us was acknowledged.

37

It was the first Wednesday of April, 1945. The officials had spent the last few days destroying all papers and documents to leave the Allies no record of what had taken place in Buchenwald. They had destroyed the list of prisoners as well, and the SS officers could no longer tell Jews from "Aryans," or the number of men in each Block, or the exact prison population.

This did not affect their plans since they intended to exterminate us all, Jews and Gentiles alike, but from the point of view of the Jews it was important since we were scheduled to go first.

We faced a desperate fight for time. If we could stay alive another week, perhaps only a day, or even an hour, the liberation armies might arrive. On their part the Nazis, too, were fighting for time, time to destroy every shred of evidence, including the prisoners, which might tell the story of Buchenwald.

The Germans thought that the Americans, once they heard the testimony of the prisoners, would stand up the entire SS, officers and men alike, and shoot them down. Had they known that affairs would drag through a long involved ten-month trial at the end of which the man who helped finance their operations would go free, perhaps they would have acted differently.

We Jews in the Big Lager decided to hide out in the "Aryan" Blocks, but before we took this step we consulted Emil. Emil had his answer ready for us.

"I've never refused to carry out an order from above in Buchenwald," he said. "At times it was a very hard and bitter thing for me to do. But it was the only way to keep men alive. Tomorrow or the next day I'm going to receive an order to lead the entire Block out to be evacuated. If I receive that order, I'm going to lead out all the men who are here. Whether you're here or not is up to you. Each one of you has to start making his own decisions immediately."

That was all. To the last moment Emil phrased his words cautiously, never taking it for granted that every listener was trustworthy. He was telling us to save ourselves by any means we could devise, and he undoubtedly knew more of the situation than any one of us. Evidently he himself intended to take the risk of leading his Block out for "evacuation" because he would not abandon those in his custody under any circumstances.

We scattered to find hiding places. It was already close to ten in the evening, and at any moment SS men might surround the Block and shoot anyone attempting to leave. Some of the "Aryan" Block Leaders to whom we went would not make room for us because they claimed we would endanger them by our presence. But two prisoner-leaders of the Underground sent messages ordering them to take us in. Then they allowed a few of us in each Block, according to what space was available.

A friend named Feuerlicht with whom I worked in the shop, decided to hide with me in the Small Lager where prisoners of every nationality were inextricably mixed. Furthermore my friend Sapir was a room attendant in one of the Small

Lager's barracks, which meant he had a small room to himself in which we might hide until morning. This was our plan, but when we arrived we found that Sapir was in the hospital, and his room was already jammed with fugitives.

The other barracks in the Small Lager were also overrun by this time since all the men from the Jewish Blocks had the same idea. Then we decided to spend the night in one of the other Blocks, and we made ourselves comfortable on a wooden bench where we proposed to sleep sitting up for a couple of hours. But at a little after ten that night another order came over the loudspeaker.

"Since the Jews disobeyed the order to report to the yard this evening, there will be a general Appel tomorrow morning at six o'clock. All prisoners must report."

This was their method of outsmarting us! No one could stay away from a general Appel without being shot down. A few minutes later another command followed:

"Jews are to line up separately."

The order to line up separately was intended for the Jews in the Small Lager who did not have separate Blocks. Feuerlicht and I put our heads together. If we went to the Jewish Block it would be impossible to avoid the Appel. If we stayed in the Small Lager we would be the victims of a thorough search for Jews among the non-Jews. We had to discover some third course of action predicated on one objective: not to report for Appel in the morning.

Together we hit upon the plan of returning to the Big Lager, but not to our Block. We decided to go to the shop where we worked. We knew every inch of the place and there were many hiding places. We were prepared to hide for two days without food, in the hope that the Americans would arrive by that time.

We started to carry out our plan, but it was not so simple. At every exit we found a Lager Schutz who was there to prevent any communication whatsoever between the Small and Big Lagers. We decided to stay where we were until four in the morning, and then attempt to steal out with the men who went to the kitchen for coffee. If successful we would be in the factory well ahead of the six o'clock Appel.

We spent the evening sitting on wooden benches and chatting with the room attendants. When the men gathered to go for coffee we stood in their rows of five and marched out with them unmolested. As we marched we could hear the rumbling of American guns again, but they sounded too far off to give promise of immediate freedom.

Feuerlicht and I went straight to our own Block where we drank coffee and pocketed our share of bread. I had been lucky enough to get a package of cigarettes. Only half the men were in the Block, the rest having found hiding places around the camp. Feuerlicht and I then set out for the shop. There was a locksmith labor gang assigned there now, but it was still too early for them to report. The shop was deserted. A prisoner guarded the entrance, but I knew him well and I explained why we were there.

"Go ahead, hide," he said. "The shop's big enough."

We climbed in through the machine-shop window. Mute machines, new equipment recently arrived, stood in the vast spaces. The furniture shop was a shambles, planks scattered about, tools lying on the floor, indicating that no work was being done there.

Beneath the flooring was a narrow basement where I had sat during air raid alarms when I worked in the shop. My friend and I forced open a door which had been nailed shut, and then descended, nailing the door again from the other side.

The cellar, however, was too obvious a place for refuge, but we knew of a trap door in one corner, flush with the floor. We raised the door. Beneath was a hole in which three or four people could sit in comfort. We collected rags and an old tattered blanket from the workshop, and with these we lined the damp underground space. Then we climbed down and drew the trap door shut over our heads. It was half past five. We sat there, determined to wait in that hole until the Americans arrived.

It was dark and airless. We munched our bread and smoked an occasional cigarette even though this still further befouled the atmosphere. We tried to doze but it was useless. We speculated on the time.

Six o'clock must have come and gone. What had happened at the Appel? How many were missing? Had those who had appeared been taken to their death as yet? We wondered, and we gasped for air in that stuffy hole. The hours passed, indistinct, monotonous, yet frightening, unmarked hours. I wondered how long we could stand this without fainting, but I wondered only to myself since I didn't want to lower my companion's morale. (He was probably asking himself the same question.)

We couldn't hear a sound above us, not a whisper, a footfall, a command. Finally we decided that when evening came we would leave the hole and go to the basement to sleep. Even if it were possible to sleep in our hiding place there would be serious danger of asphyxiation.

When we believed the evening was well advanced we clambered out of the hole and found a bench in the basement on which we stretched out to sleep. We were so thoroughly exhausted that we fell asleep immediately despite the tension and the danger. I have no idea how long we slept, but suddenly a terrific din awakened us. For a moment we thought the Americans had arrived and that a battle for the camp was in progress. Then we heard 6aths in German, French, Russian, Hungarian; the snapping of whips; the dull thud of blows, kicks; the shouting of men engaged in free-for-all fighting. The sound was coming toward the basement from the machine shop. We scuttled back to the subterranean burrow like beetles seeking shelter under a rock.

    Apparently some prisoners had hidden in the machine shop above, and the Lager police were driving them out. Since there were no shots, prisoner-guards must have been doing the job. Whatever it was, we were in the middle of it.

    Our only thought was to get out. We knew that there would be men guarding the exits after this incident, possibly Lager police whose only interest was in saving their own lives, and possibly postponing the hour of their own "evacuation."

Above us the din of the fight finally subsided. We heard the sound of planks being dragged about as though people were arranging sleeping places for themselves. Gradually this, too, ceased, and a deep silence followed.

All at once we heard sounds again, this time directly overhead. Someone was forcing the door to the basement, the same door we had nailed shut behind us. In a few moments we heard the door give, and we cautiously peered out of our hole to see who was coming. Two young men in prison garb stood near the trap door. Then two Polish Lager Schutzen appeared out of nowhere, grabbed them by the shoulders, and dragged them away. We did not believe we had been seen. We heard the police nailing the door shut after they left the basement.

Again we spent the night sitting, half-benumbed, with no room to stretch, and determined to make our way out in the morning. Our cigarettes and bread were gone but we thought of neither. We suffered most from lack of sleep. Time itself was torture, and we kept estimating, with no basis for our guesses, how long before the night would be over. At last we assumed, for no logical reason, that morning had arrived.

I raised myself up to, reach for the trap door but as I did the sound of splintering wood suddenly transfixed me, and I stood with my arm uplifted but motionless. Somebody was working on the trap door from the other side, prying at it with a fulcrum of some kind. The door shivered, then swung upward.

We looked into the faces of the two prisoners of the night before, one of whom had an iron bar in his hand. Behind them were others. Feuerlicht and I leaped out, and when they saw us they all rushed back, panic-stricken with surprise at finding us there when they feared only death from the unexpected.

My friend and I crawled out of a basement window and found ourselves in the yard opposite the locksmith's shop. Not much later the head worker of that shop, a Frenchman whom I knew well, came along and we told him our story. He led us into his shop without delay. We decided to wait there until the other workers arrived. Then the

Frenchman would give us each a box of tools and we would leave by the gate, carrying the tools as though we were on our way to do some repair job. While we waited the Frenchman told us about the previous night's Appel. "Emil led about thirty prisoners to the yard," he said, "and the Leader from the other Block led about the same number. The SS asked Emil where the others were but he just pointed at the group and said that was all there were. Even so they didn't dare "evacuate" them because they had only a few dozen soldiers on hand. Now Emil's in hiding. The others have given him orders that he's not to come out until the liberation. The Nazis are blaming him for the disappearance of the other Jews."

"What happened to those who reported?" we asked.

"Nothing as yet. They stood in the yard all day yesterday. In the evening they were placed in the carpenter shop."

In the carpenter shop—that explained the uproar we had heard during the night. The Frenchman said there was complete confusion in the camp now and that in view of the "evacuation" order, there were now officially no more Jews in Buchenwald. They had been exterminated—officially—the night before last. The Frenchman suggested that we go straight to the Small Lager when we left since there was a barracks there which the prisoner-leaders had set aside to accommodate Jews in hiding, an unofficial Jewish Barracks whose existence was unknown to the Nazis.

We took advantage of the shop's facilities to wash and shave, and then we became calmer. The Frenchman gave us each a blue workman's jacket and a box of tools. We passed the guards without question, especially since the Frenchman accompanied us to the gate and stood by our side, giving us instructions, in a clearly audible voice, as to where we were to go and what it was that needed repairing. When we reached the Small Lager, the prisoners were talking excitedly, conferring, speculating.

They gathered in groups and waited for develop-merits. On the way we passed our old barracks, the Jewish Block, and found that the Ukrainian White Guardists had taken advantage of the situation to ransack our lockers, stealing food, bits of clothing, and small luxuries such as a pipe or slippers. They remained the most despicable of ghouls to the very end!

Kurt was in charge of the special barracks set aside for us in the Small Lager, and the prisoners had organized it so well that they even managed to get a bread ration. For twenty-four hours the camp had been completely isolated from the outside world. Evidently the front had remained static. The radio was silent because the Germans had nothing good to report.

Friday, April sixth, passed uneventfully except for our waiting which was, in itself, not uneventful. We went to bed only because it had been long since we had the luxury of a narrow bunk. Loud noises woke us at four in the morning. We looked out the window. The barracks were surrounded.

38

We saw dead bodies scattered over the yard. During the night the SS had begun a large-scale "evacuation." A thousand Jews lay murdered on the stones. Those who had been unable to reach the gate were beaten to death in the yard. We heard that the most dangerous of the civilian criminals had also been eliminated. The bacchanalia of murder had recommenced!

Guards covered every barracks exit, every exit from the Small Lager. Other barracks' were in the same situation as our own, but we noticed that the prison police, the Lager Schutzen, rather than SS men, were gathering in the prisoners and turning them over in groups to the Nazis.

We planned quickly. We were not afraid of the Lager Schutzen because they were unarmed. If it became necessary to die fighting, we were all prepared to do so now. We lined up in groups of four or five, linked arms, and rushed the doors, going at the Lager Schutzen with fists, knees, boots, and sticks.

We broke through at the gates, but some among us, weakened by lack of food, were unable to fight, sank down exhausted, and were gathered up in the net.

The Lager Schutzen who received slightly augmented rations, were in better physical condition than we.

Then we ran about like hunted beasts, looking for some friendly spot where we might conceal ourselves. On every side men were running, weak, panting men with bloodshot eyes, torn clothing, splotches of blood on their bodies. We found a minute's respite behind a ruined wall. A man near me said that the order was to "evacuate" a thousand men each day.

They would soon have that number, and then we could expect quiet for a little while. As yet the Nazis had employed no weapons, machine-gunned no one, although they had to fight for each man with their whips, fists, clubs, and revolver butts.

It was evident that we could not spend the night in a barracks.

Saturday, April seventh. Another attack. No more food whatsoever. By noon the Nazis had rounded up another thousand starved, half-dead men whose battered corpses now lay in the yard. The crematorium's chimney was finally smokeless. Since it was no longer in operation the Nazis threw the dead into an enormous pit.

Night came. We slept in a ditch. The SS men were now running amok, and it was hard to tell hunter from hunted. They, too, were now fighting for their lives, but they fought unarmed, debilitated, diseased men. In our watery ditch we dozed fitfully and dreamed of the last crust of bread we had eaten on Friday.

The Nazis set aside Sunday, April eighth, for the extermination of the Russian prisoners-of-war in Buchenwald, but in this case their task was not so easily accomplished. The Russians, whose physical condition was also a little better than ours, showed no inclination to co-operate in their own extermination. They fought, wrestled, kicked, struck with stones, refusing to give up their lives cheaply. Finally the SS resorted to guns. Red soldiers lay dead in the yard and the SS, frenzied with fear, turned machine-guns on the empty Russian barracks. The battle lasted the entire day, and by nightfall the SS had succeeded in carrying out their orders despite all resistance. They forced the few thousand remaining Russians to march out to the road for the "evacuation."

The Germans had not as yet turned their attention to the hospitals, although no one was allowed to enter or leave. The children were there, and so was Emil and my friend Sapir.

On Sunday evening quiet descended again. Hundreds of Russian bodies still lay in the yard where many Red soldiers had been left to die, untended, of their wounds. We spent the evening in searching for food. Our mouths were covered with sores from hunger and thirst. We hunted high and low for a stray potato, a carrot, a crust of bread, stumbling over the bodies of the dead and dying as we searched. We did not know how much longer we could hold out, and many of us, in the last stages of starvation, simply awaited the end. One of these I recognized as Stephen Reisz, a druggist of Kolozsvar, who was lying in a semi-comatose state. I shook him to determine if he were alive. He opened his eyes and whispered, "Bread." I had none to give, and I passed on, leaving him to the merciful peace of his coma.

On Monday the Nazis renewed the attack and it lasted the entire day. I don't know how many victims they succeeded in "evacuating," but I believe it must have been about three thousand five hundred. Our power to resist was almost broken and we were actually in so depressed a state that we had to fight to retain our very will to live. Some of us no longer had the strength to continue seeking a hiding place.

The yard presented the same grisly scene as on previous nights. Killing was now easier for the SS men. We could no longer distinguish those whom the SS murdered, from those who had died of starvation. No one cleared away the corpses now.

The dull thunder of American guns came closer.

That night we investigated an abandoned cattle shed and found on the floor some half-chewed pieces of carrot which we fell on like wolves. Then we slept.

We woke up Tuesday morning, April tenth, to the loud booming of heavy artillery. The struggle began again, with most of us too far gone to care or even hide, but it only lasted until noon. Then there was a strange quiet. We staggered into the French barracks where we hoped we might find a crust of bread.

Suddenly we noticed that guards surrounded the French barracks. Prisoners from other barracks who concealed themselves there, crowded the barracks floor. I still had the strength to attempt escape, but a friend named Seszler was ready to give up. "I don't care what happens," he said. "I can't go on." He collapsed against the wall, completely beaten. I knew it would be useless to try to arouse him.

A number of us seized a blanket and waved it before us to indicate to the police outside that we were surrendering, but when we got outside the barracks gate we began to fight again. Blows flew in every direction, and I have no idea how many fell on me or even whether they caused me pain. I only know that a number of us succeeded in escaping. Two hundred meters away we were more or less safe for the moment.

At three that afternoon the "evacuation" was called off, and we discovered that our desperate battle had been unnecessary since even those who had been overpowered by the guards were not harmed.

The loudspeaker announced the cancellation of the "evacuation" but we refused to believe it. Then the two prisoner-leaders themselves confirmed the news, and we risked returning to the barracks. I went with my friends to the Belgian Block, and there we stayed.

Inside the Block I rested for a bit and then wandered around to find how many of my friends were missing. Eight days before, forty-five had been alive of the original group of us who had arrived in the transport from Belgium. Now there were twelve. Later I found that many had been taken out of the camp in the last few days, and shot. During these same eight days twenty-one thousand men were "evacuated," all of whom were murdered except for the few who had managed to escape into the woods.

On April tenth a peculiar reaction set in over the entire camp. We all gave up—all of us, prisoners and Nazis alike. Yes, the Nazis gave up. They were beaten, too. The kitchen served food. We got our Red Cross packages which contained cigarettes, chocolate, and biscuits, and within ten minutes nothing was left but the cigarettes. That day we ate the entire food supply of the camp.

At night we slept on the bunks, too tired to fight for life, and the Nazis slept, too tired for murder. No one called us from bed at four o'clock. I awoke at nine. The loudspeaker announced no Appel.

We passed the day quietly.

39

Only the roar of American planes overhead disturbed the camp's quiet on the morning of April 11, 1945. There was no alarm, no siren, no Appel whistle, and no loudspeaker. We came and went as we pleased. The guards, knowing no other duties and lacking the imagination to conceive of other actions, stood in the turrets, maintaining watch over the exhausted camp. For twenty-four hours the strident voice of the commandant, Herman Pister, was silent. Perhaps he was in hiding, crouching in the woods, cowering in the shelter of a wet ditch or behind a tree. We did not know then.

At eleven in the morning we heard a voice over the loudspeaker, but it was not the commandant's voice. It called, "Everyone inside the barracks!" The order came once, twice, then five more times.

We had regained a little strength from the food ration, strength enough to wonder whether the holocaust would begin again. What new torture had they devised? In what manner had they roused themselves from their own apathy? Were there now explosives under all the barracks, set to destroy us all? This was no far-fetched idea but one which had been tested and found efficient in other camps.

Loud gunfire accompanied the loudspeaker, and it could have been no more than a few kilometers away.

A prisoner at my side looked at me and said, "What's this? Another trap?"

"I don't know. It may be."

The camp prisoner-leaders passed from group to group in the yard and when they urged us to go into the barracks, we obeyed. But once inside we crowded around the windows to watch what was going on and to learn once and for all whether we would live, or whether our battles had been futile.

Someone looked up and shouted, "The guards have left the turrets."

A prisoner-leader ascended one of the turrets and took his place where the SS guard had stood. The telephone in the main turret rang. It was the Weimar Gauleiter calling the commandant, but one of our prisoner-officials answered the phone. "Jawohl" he said, "this is the commandant."

"All soldiers are to leave the camp at once. Put the prisoners in the barracks. Sixty sappers will arrive shortly, bringing explosives. Demolish the entire camp."

"Very good, Herr Gauleiter."

The sixty soldiers arrived, faithful to the Gauleiter's promise, coming on trucks loaded to capacity with dynamite, ready and willing to commit their last mad, useless, degenerate act before they went down in the ugliest and most sordid defeat that any people has allowed its nation to suffer. But they were too late. The prisoners had run up the white flag on the towers as a signal for the American Army, and taken over the guns and ammunition. The sixty demolition experts entered the camp with their arms over their heads.

Had they arrived a half-hour earlier, I doubt whether we would be alive today.

At one in the afternoon we looked at a new Buchenwald. Grouped at the entrance were a few Czechs, Russians, and French, and some prisoner-leaders including Emil. They were all armed. Then the loud-speaker burst out again, but this time it was a friendly voice which spoke. "Kameraden! Stay in your places! Keep discipline! It is important to keep discipline!"

And then it roared, "Kameraden, we are free!"

In the Belgian Block we were silent, stunned, and then I heard my own voice crying out, "Mes amis, nous sommes libres!"

The French and Belgians embraced, fell on one another's necks, cried, sobbed, and laughed. "Vive la liberte!" they called, and the forests of Weimar answered with an echo. Then a camp leader, speaking from the main turret, called over the loudspeaker, "Greetings and thanks to the

American Army of liberation! Kameraden, stay in your places and let us show them our discipline when they arrive! No disorder!"

And that was all.

At that moment we had in our power many Nazis including the detachment of sixty sent to blow us up. We didn't hang them. We had been surfeited with hangings, with killings, and to tell the truth we had become so used to the idea that we were the ones to wait for death, that it never occurred to us that we, too, could kill. Incredible, but that is how it was. We were too exhausted, too chronically dying, if you know what I mean, for this to matter.

At six in the evening the camp leader called us out and greeted us while American planes soared overhead, forming a huge circle as a greeting. We tried to cheer the planes but our weak voices gurgled and died in our throats.

At nine o'clock the Americans arrived and took command of the camp. They chose one prisoner to act as chief liaison man. Their choice was Emil Korlbach.

That night we slept because there was nothing else we were capable of doing. And at nine the next morning, after a good breakfast, all those whom the Americans had not hospitalized marched out to the yard. The band—it was not the Buchenwald band—played the American anthem, and then the "Internationale." Twenty thousand of us found voice to sing in twenty languages.

A few hours later the American commanding officer announced that President Roosevelt was dead.

The starry flag was lowered and we discovered that twenty thousand men who had fought suffered, starved, and fought again, could still weep. And we wept quietly there in the courtyard as the sun rose on our day of freedom.

The power and discipline of our Underground, the only organized underground in any German concentration camp, then proved itself. We did not even disturb the pen where the SS men kept the suckling pigs. We committed no anarchistic act whatsoever.

This was in marked contrast to other camps where there was no Underground and therefore no discipline, where prisoners assaulted each other after the liberation because they discovered men who had hidden away precious food. In Bergen-Belsen, for instance, a holocaust followed the liberation, a holocaust in which the prisoners slaughtered one another.

Now it is all over—or almost over. The SS is not completely dead. Nazis who worked in that camp remain alive, and their every breath travesties justice.

We are not vindictive men. We do not live by revenge, but we want justice. For the theoretical defenders of fascism, the ideologists of a "strong Germany," the enemies of "vengeance" (by which they mean "Justice"), we have nothing but the deepest contempt, the contempt for scavengers that feed off offal.

We, too, believe in a free Germany but such a Germany can only be an anti-fascist Germany. We are those who sang in the camp a song which expressed our determination that after the Nazis finally sank into the filth from which they rose, we would still be here. And we, the world anti-fascists, are here, a billion strong.